SO YOU THINK YOU'RE A CHICAGO BLACKHAWKS FAN?

STARS, STATS, RECORDS, AND MEMORIES FOR TRUE DIEHARDS

JOHN KREISER

SPORTS
PUBLISHING

Sports Publishing books may be purchased in bulk at special discounts for sales promotion, corporate gifts, fund-raising, or educational purposes. Special editions can also be created to specifications. For details, contact the Special Sales Department, Sports Publishing, 307 West 36th Street, 11th Floor, New York, NY 10018 or sportspubbooks@skyhorsepublishing.com.

Sports Publishing® is a registered trademark of Skyhorse Publishing, Inc.®, a Delaware corporation.

Visit our website at www.sportspubbooks.com.

10 9 8 7 6 5 4 3 2 1

Library of Congress Cataloging-in-Publication Data is available on file.

Cover design by Tom Lau
Cover photo credit: AP Images

ISBN: 978-1-68358-082-9
Ebook ISBN: 978-1-68358-083-6

Printed in the United States of America

Contents

Preface

A lot of my early memories of the Chicago Blackhawks (or Black Hawks, as they were known when I was young) were painful ones. As a suburban New Yorker in the pre-Internet, pre-every-game-on-TV time that was the Original Six era, I was pretty much limited to watching the Rangers—not exactly a fun thing in the early 1960s, when the Blueshirts were at one of their lowest ebbs.

The usual question for New York fans of that era wasn't whether the Rangers would make the playoffs, but rather would they finish ahead of the Boston Bruins; Chicago was one of those teams you hoped the Rangers might beat (they almost never did).

The Black Hawks always fascinated me. Those tremendous red uniforms, coupled with the fact that the ice surface at Chicago Stadium was smaller than that of other facilities (which made players like Bobby Hull seem like they were faster than they already were), added to the intrigue.

On those rare occasions when the TV station that aired Rangers games would show one from Chicago, I was captivated by the speed and power of Hull, whose shot probably did more to bring in the era of masked goalies than anything or anyone else. Stan Mikita was fascinating in a different way: He was a little guy (even by 1960s standards), and yet the puck appeared to be glued to his stick before it invariably wound up on the stick of a teammate for a good scoring chance.

(Also fascinating, as I learned years later, was that except for some power-play shifts, Hull and Mikita were rarely on the ice at the same time. But I digress . . .)

Then there was goaltender Glenn Hall. The idea that any goaltender, even in that era, could go season after season without missing a start was almost incomprehensible. I don't know what his record was against the Rangers, but to my young eyes, it seemed like they were 0–100 against him.

By the early 1970s, the Rangers were among the NHL's top teams. They met the Hawks in three consecutive Semifinals (1971–73), with Chicago winning the first and third before losing to the Montreal Canadiens in the Final both times.

The stars in Chicago have changed over the years, from Hull and Mikita to Denis Savard and Steve Larmer, to Jonathan Toews and Patrick Kane; from Pierre Pilote to Doug Wilson to Duncan Keith; from Glenn Hall to Tony Esposito to Corey Crawford. What hasn't changed is the loyalty of the fans who've always made Chicago a tough place for a visiting team.

There were some fallow years in the early part of the 21st century before executives like Dale Tallon and (later) Stan Bowman built the fabulous team that packs United Center whenever the Hawks take the ice. With three championships in a span of six seasons from 2009–10 through 2014–15, as Carly Simon might say, "These are the good old days."

I owe a debt of thanks to Julie Ganz and the folks at Skyhorse Publishing for their hard work in polishing and sanding my raw product into the finished version you hold in your hands. Special thanks to my NHL.com colleague Dave Stubbs, who answered a late call for help locating some images with his usual grace and generosity. Thanks also to my wife, Helen, for

Preface

helping me to keep my eye on the ball, er, puck as the deadlines grew closer.

Now it's time to get ready. Strap on your shin guards, sharpen your skates, and let's get started.

Introduction

For the past decade, the Chicago Blackhawks have set the standard for NHL success.

That doesn't mean they've won every Stanley Cup during that time; however, they've come closer than anyone else to becoming the first dynasty of the 21st century. Winning the Cup in 2010 ended a 49-year championship drought. Winning again in 2013 and 2015 (and coming up an overtime goal short of making the Final in 2014) cemented the Hawks' status as the NHL's best team of the early part of the new century.

The franchise's on-ice success has been matched off the ice. Under the aegis of owner Rocky Wirtz (who took over when his father, William Wirtz, died in 2007) and team president John McDonough, the Blackhawks have become one of the NHL's model franchises. The United Center is filled for every game, and millions of people have turned out for the three Stanley Cup parades. Players like Jonathan Toews, Patrick Kane, Duncan Keith, and Corey Crawford have become household names around Chicago.

All in all, it's a good time to be a Blackhawks fan.

But it's easy to forget that today's stars are building on a foundation established over the previous nine decades. Before Crawford was helping the Blackhawks win championships, there were Hall of Famers like Glenn Hall and Tony Esposito making life miserable for opposing shooters. Keith is the latest in a line of great defensemen that includes the likes of Pierre

Pilote and Doug Wilson. Toews, Kane, and Hossa have followed a line of forwards that includes 1980s stars like Denis Savard, 1960s and '70s heroes such as Bobby Hull and Stan Mikita, and even Bill Mosienko, whose 14 seasons with the Black Hawks (they didn't go to the one-word version we see today until decades later) earned him a spot in the Hockey Hall of Fame.

In addition, as much as today's fans enjoy the comforts of United Center, earlier generations savored their time at Chicago Stadium, the original "Madhouse on Madison" that was home to the Hawks from 1929 through 1994. It may not have had the amenities that United Center offers, but to generations of fans, it was home.

For nine decades, whether they've been known as the Black Hawks or Blackhawks, the Hawks have been a pillar of the National Hockey League. For the last 25 years of the Original Six era, they were the westernmost point in the NHL. In good times, and not-so-good times, they've always been among hockey's most exciting teams.

Just like a hockey game, the difficulty level of the questions you'll see will get tougher as you move along from the first period through the second and third, into overtime, and finally onto the shootout. We hope you'll have fun—and prove to your friends what a great Blackhawks fan you are!

FIRST PERIOD

The teams have made their way onto the ice. The last strains of Jim Cornelison singing the National Anthem are still echoing through United Center. The officials, two referees and two linesmen, are having their last pre-faceoff check before heading to their stations. The Blackhawks, resplendent in their red sweaters and black pants, are lining up against their white-clad opposition. The "Madhouse on Madison" is ready for another night of hockey.

The splat of the puck hitting the ice means the first period is underway . . .

1. Which Blackhawks legend appeared in the movies *Wayne's World* and *Wayne's World 2*? *Answer on page 11.*
   a) Bobby Hull
   b) Stan Mikita
   c) Tony Esposito
   d) Jeremy Roenick

2. A Chicago star of the 1950s set an NHL record that may never be broken by scoring three goals in 21 seconds in a game against the New York Rangers at Madison Square Garden on March 23, 1952. Who is he? *Answer on page 12.*
   a) Max Bentley
   b) Gus Bodnar
   c) Doug Bentley
   d) Bill Mosienko

3. It wasn't uncommon for NHL arenas built in the pre-expansion era to end up with ice surfaces that weren't the standard 200-by-85. That list includes Chicago Stadium (as well as Boston Garden, the Detroit Olympia, and Memorial Auditorium in Buffalo). Just how big was the ice surface at the Stadium? *Answer on page 14.*
   a) 188 feet long, 85 feet wide
   b) 200 feet long, 83 feet wide
   c) 196 feet long, 85 feet wide
   d) 191 feet long, 83 feet wide

4. **True or false:** The National Football League once played its championship game in Chicago Stadium (on a day the Hawks weren't there, of course). *Answer on page 15.*

5. Offense took off in the NHL during the 1970s, and there was no better example than Game 5 of the 1973 Stanley Cup Final, when the Hawks and Montreal Canadiens combined to set a single-game Final record for the most goals scored that still stands. How many goals were scored, and who won the game? *Answer on page 16.*
   a) 16 (Chicago won 9–7)
   b) 15 (Chicago won 8–7)
   c) 18 (Montreal won 10–8)
   d) 14 (Chicago won 9–5)

6. The Blackhawks' revival in the late 2000s was keyed by the arrival of center Jonathan Toews, who was selected in the first round (No. 3) of the 2006 NHL Draft. Toews had finished his freshman year of college when he was drafted and opted to stay there for one more season before joining the Hawks in 2007. At which college did Toews play? *Answer on page 17.*

7. The Vezina Trophy used to be given to the goalies on the team who allowed the fewest goals in the regular season; it was later changed to an award given to the goaltender voted to be the best in the NHL. Only one Blackhawks goaltender has won the Vezina under its current format. Who is he? *Answer on page 18.*

8. Patrick Kane set a franchise record in 2015–16 when he had at least one point in 26 consecutive games. Which Hall of Famer held the previous team record with a 21-game point streak? *Answer on page 19.*
a) Stan Mikita
b) Bobby Hull
c) Doug Bentley
d) Bill Mosienko

9. Joel Quenneville moved into second place on the NHL's all-time list for coaching victories when the Blackhawks defeated the Montreal Canadiens 2–1 on January 14, 2016. The man he passed won the Stanley Cup with Chicago as a player. Who was he? *Answer on page 19.*

10. Bobby Hull set off one of the biggest eruptions in the history of Chicago Stadium on March 12, 1966, when he became the first player ever in the NHL to score more than 50 goals in a season. He scored his record-setting 51st goal on a power-play slap shot in the third period. Against which team did he score goal No. 51? You get a bonus point for naming the goaltender! *Answer on page 21.*

11. How many goals did Bobby Hull score in his highest goal-scoring season? *Answer on page 22.*
a) 52 goals
b) 54 goals

c) 58 goals

d) 61 goals

12. Which team drafted forward Marian Hossa, a key to Chicago's championship teams in 2010, 2013, and 2015? In which year, round, and overall draft position was he taken? *Answer on page 23.*

13. Which of these is NOT true about Blackhawks star Patrick Kane? *Answer on page 25.*
   a) He was the first player taken in the 2007 NHL Draft.
   b) He's the first US-born player to win the Art Ross Trophy.
   c) He scored the overtime goal that won the Stanley Cup in 2010.
   d) He led the NHL with 50 goals in 2015–16.

14. Which college did defenseman Duncan Keith play for prior to joining the Blackhawks? *Answer on page 26.*
   a) Michigan State
   b) Michigan
   c) Notre Dame
   d) Lake Superior State

15. Artemi Panarin won the Calder Trophy as the NHL's top rookie in 2015–16, leading all first-year players in goals (30), assists (47), and points (77). He also joined Sidney Crosby as the only NHL rookie since 1993–94 to accomplish something else. What was it? *Answer on page 27.*
   a) 10-game point streak
   b) 10 game-winning goals
   c) 10 games with three or more points
   d) 10-game assist streak

16. Who holds the Blackhawks record for most consecutive seasons leading the team in points? *Answer on page 28.*
a) Stan Mikita
b) Jeremy Roenick
c) Denis Savard
d) Paul Thompson

17. Which of these Blackhawks was not a first-round draft pick? *Answer on page 29.*
a) Duncan Keith
b) Marian Hossa
c) Brent Seabrook
d) Jonathan Toews

18. How many times has Jonathan Toews scored 30 or more goals? *Answer on page 30.*
a) Once
b) Twice
c) Three times
d) Never

19. The Blackhawks pulled off one of the great comebacks of all time to win Game 6 of the 2013 Stanley Cup Final, rallying from a 2–1 deficit for a 3–2 victory with two goals late in the third period. Who scored the game-tying and Cup-winning goals? *Answer on page 31.*

20. Denis Savard holds the Blackhawks record for 100-point seasons with five. Who is the only other Chicago player to finish with 100 points in a season more than once? *Answer on page 33.*
a) Bobby Hull
b) Stan Mikita
c) Jeremy Roenick
d) Patrick Kane

21. Bobby Hull left the Hawks after the 1971–72 season as the owner of the NHL career record for hat tricks. How many did he have? *Answer on page 35.*
a) 24
b) 28
c) 30
d) 32

22. Only one player in Chicago's 90 NHL seasons has scored on a penalty shot in a Stanley Cup Playoff game—and he's done it twice. Who is he? *Answer on page 36.*
a) Michael Frolik
b) Patrick Kane
c) Stan Mikita
d) Denis Savard

23. Goaltender Corey Crawford had a career-high seven shutouts for the Blackhawks in the 2015–16 season. How many of those shutouts came at the United Center? *Answer on page 38.*
a) 0
b) 2
c) 4
d) 7

24. Forward Andrew Ladd, a member of the Blackhawks' 2010 championship team, had won the Stanley Cup before he came to Chicago. With which team did he win it? *Answer on page 39.*
a) Anaheim Ducks
b) Carolina Hurricanes
c) Detroit Red Wings
d) Pittsburgh Penguins

25. Patrick Kane led the NHL in scoring in 2015–16. He was tops on the Blackhawks in seven of eight key offensive categories. In which category was he not No. 1? *Answer on page 41.*
a) Power-play goals
b) Shorthanded goals
c) Game-winning goals
d) Shots on goal

26. Kane also won the Hart Trophy as the NHL's most valuable player in 2015–16. How many Blackhawks had won the trophy before Kane? *Answer on page 42.*
a) 2
b) 4
c) 6
d) 8

27. From their first season in 1926–27 through 2016–17, the Black Hawks/Blackhawks list 34 players who've been officially designated as captain. But which player has worn the "C" longer than anyone else in franchise history? *Answer on page 44.*

28. Three players have scored more than 400 goals wearing a Blackhawks uniform. Two of them are Hockey Hall of Famers Stan Mikita and Bobby Hull. Who is the third? *Answer on page 45.*
a) Steve Larmer
b) Denis Savard
c) Patrick Kane
d) Dennis Hull

29. Four players have dressed for at least 1,000 games with the Hawks. Who are they? *Answer on page 47.*

30. A piece of history came to an end in 1975 when a change was made to Chicago Stadium. What was it? *Answer on page 48.*

31. The Blackhawks have had a number of the NHL's most memorable forward lines during their nine decades in the NHL. Which threesome had the most goals and points in one season? *Answer on page 49.*

32. In 1964, five Hawks were named First-Team All-Stars. Who were they, and which Hall of Famer was the lone non-Hawk on the team? *Answer on page 50.*

33. Since 1990, the Blackhawks have had just one season in which they didn't have at least one shutout. When was that season? *Answer on page 51.*
a) 1992–93
b) 1996–97
c) 2011–12
d) 2014–15

34. How many sub-.500 seasons has Blackhawks coach Joel Quenneville had? *Answer on page 52.*
a) 0
b) 1
c) 2
d) 4

35. Which of these teams was never a primary minor league affiliate of the Blackhawks? *Answer on page 52.*
a) Dallas Black Hawks
b) Saginaw Hawks
c) New Brunswick Hawks
d) Chicago Wolves

36. What injury or illness forced goaltender Corey Crawford to miss 10 consecutive games during the 2016–17 season? *Answer on page 54.*
a) Flu
b) Herniated disc
c) Appendicitis
d) Broken foot

37. Which player holds the franchise records for the fastest two goals and fastest three goals in a playoff game? *Answer on page 55.*
a) Dick Redmond
b) Bobby Hull
c) Dennis Hull
d) Jeremy Roenick

38. Two Blackhawks have scored multiple hat tricks in the same playoff year. Who are they? *Answer on page 56.*

39. Marian Hossa scored his 500th NHL goal on October 19, 2016. Who was the goaltender who allowed Hossa's milestone goal? *Answer on page 57.*
a) Steve Mason (Flyers)
b) Michal Neuvirth (Flyers)
c) Jake Allen (Blues)
d) Carter Hutton (Blues)

40. The Hawks would have a few more Stanley Cups if they had been able to get past a particular team in the Final. Which opponent has beaten Chicago in all five meetings in the Final? *Answer on page 58.*
a) Toronto Maple Leafs
b) Detroit Red Wings

c) Montreal Canadiens
d) Boston Bruins

There's the horn that ends the first period. Time to head back to the dressing room, grab some refreshment, and get ready for period No. 2.

FIRST PERIOD—ANSWERS

1. b. Stan Mikita is in the Hockey Hall of Fame because he was one of the greatest players of his era, a slick scorer and passer whose 541 goals are still second on Chicago's all-time list. He spent more than two decades as a member of the Blackhawks, and if there were a Mount Rushmore for Hawks players, his would be one of the faces on it.

But in the early 1990s, he became known to a whole new generation of fans—movie fans, that is. Much of the action in *Wayne's World* and *Wayne's World 2* takes place at "Stan Mikita's Donuts," a fictional coffee shop in Aurora, Illinois, modeled after Tim Hortons, the popular donut chain. But the *Wayne's World* version had a 12-foot statue of Mikita in full Hawks gear on the roof.

Mikita's involvement with the movie began with a phone call from Paramount Pictures. "A woman said that Mike Myers (a Toronto Maple Leafs and Stan Mikita fan) and Lorne Michaels are doing this movie and they're wondering if they can use my image and name," Mikita told writer Anne B. Stein. "I said, 'Yeah, but by the way, don't you want me in the movie? What am I, chopped liver?'"

Of course, one of the ironies is that Mikita spent much of his career going up against Horton, a Hall of Fame defenseman who helped the Toronto Maple Leafs win four Stanley Cups in the 1960s. They didn't even look much alike: Horton was a solid, wide-bodied defender; Mikita was the prototype of a skilled, shifty center.

Stan Mikita was among the former Hawks who celebrated the team's Stanley Cup championships in 2010, 2013, and 2015.

But the fictional "Stan Mikita's Donuts" was brought to life during the NHL's 2017 All-Star Weekend. From January 27–29, it was set up at Los Angeles Convention Center. Fans who made their way into the pop-up donut shop got a look at some actual Mikita memorabilia as well as items from the set of *Wayne's World*.

2. d. The Hawks were already assured of finishing last in the six-team NHL in 1951–52 when they came to Madison Square Garden for their season finale against the fifth-place New York Rangers. The home side appeared to be on the way to an easy victory, leading 6–2 with less than 14 minutes remaining in the game. But that was before Chicago center Bill Mosienko scored the fastest hat trick in NHL history.

Mosienko beat Rangers goaltender Lorne Anderson at 6:09, 6:20, and 6:30 (and almost scored again right off the next faceoff, but his shot hit the post). Mosienko's record-setting hat trick keyed Chicago's rally, which turned a four-goal deficit into a 7–6 victory.

"That record will never be broken. Never," Hall of Fame teammate Bill Gadsby said. "It was just fantastic, it was near the same play off the faceoff each one. He could really skate. He could really fly and he scored those three goals. I mean, it was unbelievable just to watch it!"

It was an achievement Mosienko never forgot.

"It was quite an accomplishment, I hope [the record] stays," he said afterwards. "After I scored the third goal, Jim Peters skated up to me and told me to keep the puck because I had set a new record. I was very happy and proud. It was like being on cloud nine."

The fact that Mosienko even wound up with Chicago was amazing enough. Joe Cooper, a Hawks player, saw Mosienko skating on an outdoor rink in Winnipeg and recommended that the team sign him. He signed with Chicago as an 18-year-old. Mosienko scored his first two NHL goals on February 9, 1942—21 seconds apart.

Though he's best known for the NHL's fastest hat trick, Mosienko's superb career earned him induction into the Hockey Hall of Fame in 1965. In his 14-year career, which was spent exclusively with the Hawks, Mosienko had 258 goals and 282 assists—big offensive numbers in an era when scoring wasn't easy and seasons were shorter. He won the

Lady Byng Trophy in 1945 as the NHL's most sportsmanlike player, and finished his career with 121 penalty minutes in 710 games.

Linemate Gus Bodnar set a record of his own by assisting on all three goals, giving him the fastest three assists in NHL history.

3. a. If you ever attended a game at the Stadium (or saw one on television), you'll probably remember that the neutral zone looked very small. That's because it was: The ice surface matched the NHL's standard width (85 feet), but it was just 188 feet long, a full 12 feet shorter than the league's standard of 200 feet (all current NHL arenas are 200-by-85). The missing ice was taken out of the neutral zone, making the Stadium ideal for a close-checking, bruising team.

The shorter ice also meant that big shooters like Bobby Hull got to the attacking zone a stride or two faster at home, making life tougher for opposing checkers and goalies.

Playing on a non-standard rink can give you a pretty nice home-ice advantage: The Blackhawks were 1,113–720–340 (.590) in their 2,173 regular-season games at Chicago Stadium and outscored their opponents 7,327–5.989.

Strangely enough, Chicago Stadium was not the only non-standard arena in the post-expansion era of the NHL.

The Olympia, home of the Detroit Red Wings until midway through the 1979–80 season, was 200 feet long but just 83 feet wide, two feet narrower than regulation. Memorial Auditorium in Buffalo was 85 feet wide but just 196 feet long. Boston Garden, which opened five years earlier than the Stadium and housed the Bruins until 1995, was both narrow and short, measuring 191 feet long and 83 feet wide.

As the old arenas died off, so did non-standard rink sizes. All 30 ice surfaces used by NHL teams during the 2016–17 season were 200-by-85.

4. Strangely enough, the Stadium did indeed host a football game (this was long before the days of arena football). The Chicago Bears and Portsmouth Spartans were set to play for the NFL championship on December 18, 1932, at Wrigley Field after finishing with identical 6–1 records (at the time, ties were discarded and not all teams played the same number of games). But the weather didn't cooperate: Chicago was gripped in subzero temperatures, and Wrigley Field had waist-high snowdrifts after being hit by blizzards.

Two days before the game was scheduled to be played, the teams agreed to move it to the Stadium. Playing football at the Stadium wasn't unheard of: Two years earlier, the Bears and Chicago (now Arizona) Cardinals had played a charity exhibition game; the game was moved indoors primarily to make sure there would be adequate attendance and gate revenue.

Because of the shorter field (60 yards long, plus end zones; 45 yards wide, covered with six inches of dirt), there were some rule changes. The sidelines were butted up against the stands. The goalposts were moved from the end lines to the goal lines (this later became standard in the NFL for decades). The ball was automatically moved back 20 yards every time one team crossed the 10-yard line, and for the first time, all plays started with the ball on or between the hash marks, which were 10 yards from the sidelines. In addition, neither team was allowed to attempt drop kicks and field goals.

For the first three quarters, the Bears and Spartans might as well have been playing on ice; that's how bad the footing was. The game was scoreless through three quarters before the Bears went ahead on a touchdown pass from Bronko Nagurski to Red Grange. The Bears also got a safety when the Spartans fumbled the ball out of the end zone.

The game was played in front of 11,198 fans, who were undoubtedly warmer inside the Stadium than they would have been in the 20-degree temperature outside.

5. b. The fans who packed the Montreal Forum for Game 5 of the 1973 Final expected to see the Canadiens finish off the Hawks and win their second Stanley Cup in three seasons. Instead, they saw the wildest game ever played in the Final.

The Canadiens took a quick 1–0 lead, but goals by Dennis Hull and Stan Mikita put the Hawks ahead 2–1. A power-play goal by Peter Mahovlich with 5:08 remaining in the first period sent the teams to their dressing rooms tied 2–2.

Montreal took three one-goal leads in the second period, but the Hawks pulled even each time on goals by Dave Kryskow, Mikita, and Jim Pappin. In a total of 31:24 playing time, the NHL's two best teams had combined for 10 goals.

But the offensive fireworks didn't stop.

A power-play goal by low-scoring defenseman Len Frig (set up by Mikita) at 16:21 put Chicago ahead 6–5, and Pappin scored his second of the night at 19:03 for a 7–5 lead after two periods.

Defenseman Serge Savard got the Canadiens within a goal when he scored 1:15 into the third period, but a goal by center Lou Angotti (another player known more as a checker than a scorer) at 4:05 restored Chicago's two-goal advantage. It proved to be the game-winner when Henri Richard scored midway through the third period to make it a one-goal game again.

The 15 combined goals in Chicago's 8–7 victory are still the most in a Stanley Cup Final game.

Amazingly, those 15 goals came against two Hall of Fame goalies: Tony Esposito of the Hawks and Ken Dryden of the Canadiens. Even more amazing: The 15 goals were scored on a total of 60 shots on goal (30 by each team).

Nor were the big scoring numbers bolstered by a lot of power-play goals. Each team had just one opportunity with the extra man. Chicago scored on its power-play chance; the Canadiens got a goal just as a penalty to Christian Bordeleau expired.

Mikita and Pappin each scored twice for Chicago. Mikita also had two assists for a four-point night. Claude Larose was the only Montreal player to score twice.

Ironically, the offensive outburst came just two days after the Hawks came up empty in Game 4, losing 4–0 at Chicago Stadium.

6. The Blackhawks drafted Jonathan Toews after he had helped the University of North Dakota reach the NCAA Frozen Four in his freshman year. Toews stayed at UND for another season, finishing with 46 points (18 goals, 28 assists) in 34 games to help North Dakota return to the Frozen Four. However, he opted to skip his final two seasons and signed a three-year, entry-level contract with Chicago on May 16, 2007.

But just because Toews left school after two years didn't mean his impact left with him.

In 2015, Nick Schmaltz, Chicago's first-round pick in the 2014 NHL Draft, told ESPN.com that while he didn't go to UND only because Toews went there, it didn't hurt.

"It's pretty cool," Schmaltz said. "It's obviously cool he was here and now he's on the Blackhawks. There's a lot of other great alumni who have been here. I just came here because of the tradition and I know how well they develop players. That was the biggest thing for me."

For his part, Toews told ESPN the fact that his name was still being heard inside Ralph Engelstad Arena was significant.

"That means a lot," Toews said. "I think those are important years in your career. For me, I had a great experience at North Dakota. We didn't win a championship. We were very close two years in a row. That was a tough one to leave behind especially when you're with great friends and good teammates.

"I think for me it was a great place for me to go to and develop and step up and have a chance to play in the NHL. Obviously, it means a lot. I've had an eventful career so far, and they definitely have their place in the contribution to that."

7. The Vezina Trophy was donated in honor of Montreal Canadiens goaltender Georges Vezina, who posted the first shutout in NHL history and died from tuberculosis.

Glenn Hall and Tony Esposito took home the Vezina three times each when it was given to the goalie(s) on the team that allowed the fewest goals.

But after the Vezina was changed to the current format (best goaltender) beginning in the 1981–82 season, the only Chicago goalie to win the trophy was Ed Belfour. He did it in 1990–91 and again in 1992–93.

"There's no doubt in my mind he's the best goaltender in the league this year," his coach, Mike Keenan, said before the NHL announced its awards after the 1990–91 season. "That has been established by his numbers in every department—his goals-against average, his win percentage, the number of wins that he's had in the league."

Perhaps most amazing about Belfour's play in 1990–91 is that he came to training camp as a 25-year-old rookie with just 23 previous NHL games prior to Keenan's arrival. Belfour was one of five goaltenders vying for two spots. He was up against veterans Greg Millen and Jacques Cloutier, prospect Jimmy Waite, and Czechoslovak import Dominik Hasek, regarded as the best goaltender in Europe.

As it turned out, the Blackhawks traded Cloutier and sent Waite and Hasek to the minors (Hasek was eventually traded to the Buffalo Sabres). Belfour took over as the starter, with Millen serving as a rarely used backup.

8. b. Kane's 26-game streak blew past the previous mark set by Bobby Hull from December 5, 1971, to January 23, 1972. Kane's streak was the longest in the NHL since Mats Sundin, then with the Quebec Nordiques, had a 30-gamer in 1992–93. He had 40 points (16 goals, 24 assists) during the streak, which was also the longest in NHL history by a US-born player.

Kane's production during the streak was a major reason that he cruised to the NHL scoring championship with 106 points.

9. Al Arbour never coached the Hawks, but as a defenseman, he was a member of the 1961 Cup-winning team. Best known as the first NHL blueliner to play while wearing glasses, Arbour was the personification of a defensive defenseman; he played three seasons with the Hawks (1958–61) and contributed six goals and 23 points in 180 regular-season games.

Arbour played seven games for the Hawks during the 1961 Stanley Cup Playoffs and was a part of the team that brought the NHL championship back to Chicago. But just as he had come to the Hawks when they claimed him in the intraleague draft in 1958, he left Chicago when the Toronto Maple Leafs claimed him the same way three years later.

The move turned out to be a good one for Arbour, whose style of play meshed perfectly with the way the Leafs played. Arbour spent all of the 1961–62 season with Toronto and dressed for eight games in the Leafs' run to the Cup. He spent most of the next two seasons in the minors, but was called up in time to play in one playoff game in 1964, getting his name on the Cup for the fourth time.

Arbour didn't get back into the NHL on a full-time basis until the 1967 expansion, when the St. Louis Blues selected him. He spent the next three-plus seasons as a player with the Blues, then had a couple of stints as their coach before being hired by the second-year New York Islanders in 1973.

Arbour had the Islanders within one game of a trip to the Stanley Cup Final in his second season behind the bench on Long Island, and they were among the NHL's most successful teams through the rest of the 1970s. They took the next step in 1980 by winning the Cup, then became a dynasty by winning in each of the next three seasons as well. Arbour coached them to the Final in 1984, but they lost to the Edmonton Oilers.

He stepped down as coach after the 1985–86 season, but returned early in 1988–89 and coached the Islanders through the 1993–94 season. He made a one-game return in November 2007 to give him exactly 1,500 games behind the bench with the Islanders.

Arbour finished his career with 782 victories, and he was second to Scotty Bowman (1,244) until Quenneville passed him on January 14, 2016. Quenneville surpassed 850 career victories during the 2016–17 season, but he still has a long way to go to catch Bowman.

10. For two periods, it looked like the New York Rangers were going to spoil the night for the crowd that packed Chicago Stadium in the hope that they would see Hull make history by becoming the first player in the NHL to score more than 50 goals, a total previously reached only by Maurice Richard in 1944–45, Bernie "Boom Boom" Geoffrion in 1960–61, and Hull himself in 1961–62.

The Rangers shut down Hull and the rest of the Hawks through the first 40 minutes and took a 2–0 lead into the third period. But with the packed house at fever pitch, the Hawks stepped up their game.

Hull assisted on Chico Maki's goal at 2:57 of the third period to make it 2–1. Less than three minutes later, Hull raced over the New York blue line, came almost to a stop about 40 feet from the net, and teed up a slap shot. Teammate Eric Nesterenko was screening Rangers goaltender Cesare Maniago and got out of the way an instant before the puck hit the back of the net, putting Hull all alone in the record book.

"I moved the puck out front for the slap shot," Hull remembered. "I got it out too far and almost topped it, didn't get real good wood on the thing and it skidded away, skimming the ice. I watched it all the way into the corner of the net. I'll never forget the ovation."

That's not surprising: Hull received a 10-minute ovation that was so loud he later admitted that he had goose bumps.

In the March 21, 1966, issue of *Sports Illustrated*, Martin Kane wrote:

"When the red light that signifies a goal flashed on, the 20,000 fans in the stadium lost control. They littered the ice with debris that ranged from hats—both men's and women's—to confetti. As he skated toward the Black Hawk bench, Hull picked up one of the more ludicrous hats and put it on, getting a laugh because, after all, he was Bobby Hull and no man in the history of the National Hockey League, give or take 50-game or 70-game seasons, had ever made such a goal before."

Ironically, Maniago had also given up Geoffrion's 50th goal five years earlier while playing for the Toronto Maple Leafs.

The power-play goal at 5:34 also tied the game 2–2, and Hull assisted on Maki's go-ahead goal less than two minutes later. In all, the Hawks scored four times in the third period and won 4–2.

But Hull wasn't finished. He scored three more goals before the end of the season to finish with 54 in a 70-game season. He also won the Art Ross Trophy as the NHL's leading scorer with 97 points, another record, and took home the Hart Trophy as the most valuable player.

11. c. It's amazing to look back to the 1960s and early 1970s and contemplate what Bobby Hull was able to accomplish. Despite playing most of his career in an era when defense and goaltending ruled the NHL, Hull was able to fill the net like no one before him.

Hull became the third player in NHL history to score 50 goals in a season in 1961–62, joining Maurice Richard and Bernie "Boom Boom" Geoffrion, each of whom did it while playing for the Montreal Canadiens.

Four years later, "The Golden Jet" became the first player in NHL history to score more than 50 goals in a season. He got No. 51 on March 12, 1966, and finished the season with 54, a total that many experts thought might never be topped.

But "never" in this case was only three years. After Hull led the league with 44 goals in 1966–67 and 52 in 1967–68, he had a career year (at least as far as his time in the NHL was concerned) by tearing up opposing defenses for 58 goals in 1968–69. Hull's performance was a big reason the Hawks finished second in the NHL with 280 goals (he also had 49 assists to finish with a league-high 107 points, meaning that he was directly involved in nearly 40 percent of Chicago's goals); however, Chicago also finished last in the East Division (albeit with a winning record).

Injuries helped limit Hull to 61 games and 38 goals in 1969–70, but he bounced back with 44 in 1970–71 to help Chicago advance to the Stanley Cup Final, and reached 50 goals in 1971–72, which turned out to be his final NHL season until 1979–80—he was the first major signing by the new World Hockey Association in the summer of 1972.

Hull's 58 goals are still a single-season record for the Hawks.

12. Marian Hossa seems like such an institution in Chicago that it's easy to forget he had a stellar career before he ever set foot in the home dressing room at United Center. The Blackhawks are his fifth NHL team, and the only one he's played with for 500 or more games.

Hossa was a smash with Dukla Trencin in Slovakia's top league in 1996–97, finishing with 44 points (25 goals, 19 assists). That was enough to convince the Ottawa Senators to take him with the 12th choice in the first round of the 1997 NHL Draft.

The Senators brought Hossa to North America for training camp prior to the 1997–98 season, but after he managed just one assist in seven games, Ottawa sent him to the Portland Winter Hawks of the Western Hockey League, which had acquired

Hossa's junior rights. He spent the rest of the season ripping up the WHL, finishing with 85 points (45 goals, 40 assists) in 53 games, then contributed 19 points (13 goals, six assists) to help Portland win the WHL championship and Memorial Cup.

A knee injury sustained in the Memorial Cup title game hampered his play in 1998–99, his first NHL season. But he scored 29 goals in 1999–2000, then had 32 and 31 in his next two seasons before putting up a career-high 45 goals in 2002–03.

Marian Hossa scored his 500th NHL goal during the 2016-17 season.

But after the 2004–05 NHL lockout kept him in Europe for a season, Hossa returned for 2005–06 and was traded to the Atlanta Thrashers. He had 43 goals and 92 points in his first season in Atlanta, then scored 43 goals and finished with 100 points in 2006–07, helping the Thrashers advance to the Stanley Cup Playoffs for the first time.

The Thrashers dealt him to the Pittsburgh Penguins prior to the NHL Trade Deadline in 2007–08; he helped Pittsburgh get to the Stanley Cup Final by putting up 26 points (12 goals, 14 assists) in 20 playoff games. In hopes of playing on a Cup-winning team, Hossa signed with the Red Wings in the summer of 2009, but after scoring 40 goals during the regular season, Hossa again came out on the losing side when the Penguins won Game 7 in the Final at Detroit.

On July 1, 2009, Hossa signed a 12-year contract with Chicago. His offensive numbers aren't what they were earlier in his career, and he was forced to miss the 2017-18 season because of a skin condition, but Hossa's two-way game helped the Hawks win the Cup in 2010, 2013, and 2015.

13. d. Patrick Kane has been one of the linchpins of the Blackhawks' revival ever since he was taken with the No. 1 pick in the 2007 NHL Draft.

Kane was an instant success in Chicago, finishing with 72 points (21 goals, 51 assists) in 2007–08 and winning the Calder Trophy as the NHL's top rookie. After a 25-goal, 70-point season in 2008–09, Kane was a First-Team All-Star selection in 2009–10, when he scored 30 goals for the first time in his NHL career and had 58 assists for 88 points.

He was even better during the Stanley Cup Playoffs, finishing with 28 points (10 goals, 18 assists) in 22 games to help the Hawks win their first championship since 1961. By far his most important goal was his last one; Kane's shot at 4:06 of overtime in Game 6 beat Flyers goaltender Michael Leighton to give the Hawks the Cup.

Kane continued to be one of the NHL's most consistent point producers for the next five seasons (four full seasons and the 48-game lockout-shortened 2012–13 seasons). He scored 23 to 27 goals in each season and finished with 64–73 points in the four full seasons as well as 55 in 47 games in 2012–13.

After finishing with 64 points in 61 games during 2014–15 before a broken leg in late February ended his regular season, Kane bounced back in the playoffs with 23 points (11 goals, 12 assists) in 23 games to fuel the Hawks' run to a third Stanley Cup in six seasons.

Everything came together for Kane during the 2015–16 season. He had a career year with a league-leading 106 points. He became the first US-born player to win the Art Ross Trophy as well as the Hart and Ted Lindsay trophies. Kane's 46 goals were also a career high; he finished four behind Alex Ovechkin of the Washington Capitals for the Maurice Richard Trophy, given to the NHL's leading goal scorer.

14. a. Duncan Keith has been the cornerstone of the Hawks' defense since making his debut with Chicago during the 2005–06 season. He was a part of the Stanley Cup-winning teams in 2010, 2013, and 2015, and is a two-time winner of the Norris Trophy, given to the NHL's top defenseman.

Keith switched from forward to defense at age 10. After tearing up minor hockey, he earned a spot on the Penticton Panthers (now the Penticton Vees) of the British Columbia Hockey League.

Unlike players in the Canadian Hockey League, BCHL players are eligible to compete for US college hockey programs. Not surprisingly, Keith was heavily recruited after finishing with 82 points (18 goals, 64 assists) in 60 games during his second season with Penticton. He finally opted to play at Michigan State.

Keith scored three goals and finished with 15 points in 2001–02, his first season with the Spartans—not huge offensive numbers, but enough to persuade the Blackhawks to take him in the second round (No. 54) of the 2002 NHL Draft.

He scored three goals and had nine points in 15 games for Michigan State at the start of the 2002–03 season before opting to join the Kelowna Rockets of the Western Hockey League. Keith's offensive game flourished at Kelowna, where he had 46 points (11 goals, 35 assists) in 37 games, then helping the Rockets win the WHL title and advance to the Memorial Cup.

Keith signed with the Hawks during the summer of 2003 and spent the next two seasons developing his game at the AHL level with the Norfolk Admirals before making his NHL debut on October 5, 2005.

15. c. Artemi Panarin was a wonderful surprise to Hawks fans in 2015–16. Chicago signed him after he put up 62 points (26 goals, 36 assists) in 54 games with SKA St. Petersburg of the Kontinental Hockey League in Russia. He also helped Russia win the 2011 IIHF World Junior Championship and sparked SKA to the Gagarin Cup (Russia's equivalent of the Stanley Cup) in 2015.

Panarin won the Calder Trophy as the NHL's top rookie in 2015–16 by putting up 77 points (30 goals, 47 assists) in 80 games.

Panarin's longest point streak was only six games (Nov. 6–18) and his longest assist streak was just three games. He did score seven game-winning goals.

But perhaps his most impressive stat is this: Panarin had three or more points in 10 of his 80 games. He and Sidney Crosby (2005–06) are the only NHL rookies since 1993–94 to reach double figures in three-point games.

16. c. There's a temptation to think that Stan Mikita would hold the mark for most consecutive seasons leading the Hawks in scoring. After all, he's the all-time franchise leader in goals and points.

But Mikita's longest streak of leading Chicago in scoring was just three seasons: 1962–65. Mikita topped the Hawks with 76 points in 1962–63, then led the NHL in scoring in 1963–64 with 89 points and again in 1964–65 with 87. Mikita led Chicago in scoring on five other occasions, but never more than twice in a row.

The biggest reason Mikita's streak wasn't longer can be summed up in two words: Bobby Hull. He ended Mikita's three-year run by leading the NHL with 97 points in 1965–66, snapped Mikita's two-year run by piling up 107 points in 1968–69, and won again in 1970–71 (96 points) and 1971–72 (93).

Jeremy Roenick was part of some of the highest-scoring teams in franchise history. He led the Hawks in scoring in three consecutive seasons, finishing with 103 points in 1991–92 and 107 in each of the next two seasons. However, he never came close to those numbers again in a career that lasted until 2008–09.

Paul Thompson is largely forgotten today, but he was the Hawks' best offensive player of the 1930s. He led Chicago in scoring for six consecutive seasons, beginning in 1932–33 (33 points) through 1937–38 (a team-record 44 points). Thompson was the top regular-season scorer on the Hawks' first two Stanley Cup-winning teams in 1934 and 1938.

But no Hawk dominated the team scoring race the way Denis Savard did during the 1980s. After finishing with 75 points in 1980–81, his rookie season, Savard became one of the most spectacular offensive players in the NHL. He led the Hawks in points in each of the next seven seasons and broke the 100-point mark five times, capped by his team-record 131 points in 1987–88.

In all, Savard piled up 1,096 points (377 goals, 719 assists) in 881 games with Chicago before being traded to his hometown Montreal Canadiens on June 29, 1990.

17. a. The Hawks had some big hits in the first round of the NHL Draft in the first decade of the 21st century. Brent Seabrook (2003), Jonathan Toews (2006), and Patrick Kane (2007) have been cornerstones of Chicago's excellence during the past decade.

They've also brought in first-rounders from other teams, most notably Marian Hossa, who was signed in the summer of 2009, more than a decade after being taken with the 12th selection in the first round of the 1997 draft.

But elite teams are built with more than first-round picks. For the Hawks, there's no better example than two-time Norris Trophy-winning defenseman Duncan Keith.

Chicago picked Russian defenseman Anton Babchuk in the first round (No. 21) of the 2002 NHL Draft. Babchuk played 289 games in the NHL, just 22 with the Hawks. It might not be fair to label Babchuk a bust, but it's certainly fair to say that they expected more from a first-round pick.

Luckily for the Hawks, they selected Keith in the second round (No. 54). Keith has been a pillar of strength on defense for more than a decade and won the Conn Smythe Trophy as playoff MVP in 2015.

(The Hawks also scored big in the second round of the next two drafts. In 2003, they followed the selection of Seabrook in the first round by taking goaltender Corey Crawford in round two (No. 52). One year later, taking useful forwards Dave Bolland and Bryan Bickell in the second round helped to make up for taking defenseman Cam Barker with the third pick in the first round).

18. b. Jonathan Toews has been one of the NHL's most consistent scorers since arriving in Chicago for the 2007–08 season. He's had at least 21 goals in every season (including 2012–13, which was shortened to 48 games by a lockout). In the six seasons he's played 75 or more games, Toews has scored at least 25 goals.

However, Toews has exceeded 30 goals just twice in those 10 seasons.

In 2008–09, his second NHL season and his first after being named captain, Toews played all 82 games and bumped up his goal production to 34 from the 24 he scored as a rookie. Toews connected for 12 power-play goals and had seven game-winners, helping the Blackhawks return to the Stanley Cup Playoffs for the first time since 2002.

Toews missed six games in 2009–10 because of concussion-like symptoms and dropped to 25 goals (though he had an NHL career-best 43 assists and finished with 68 points). Toews also scored seven goals and finished with 29 points in 22 playoff games, helping the Hawks end a 49-year Cup drought.

The Hawks needed more offense from Toews in 2010–11, when the salary cap forced them to trade off several key players from their Cup-winning team. He stepped up with 32 goals (his second 30-goal season) and a career-best 76 points. Toews had 10 power-play goals and eight game-winners. He showed off his all-around game as well, finishing with a plus-25 rating and winning 56.7 percent of his faceoffs.

Injuries limited Toews to 59 games in 2011–12 and were the reason he came up just short of his third 30-goal season. Toews finished with 29 goals and 57 points despite missing 23 games. He was healthy again during the lockout-shortened 2012–13 season and had 48 points (23 goals, 25 assists) in 47 games.

Toews had 28 goals in each of the next three seasons. He continued to score in the clutch, producing a total of 20 game-winning goals and connecting five times in overtime in 2015–16.

Midseason injuries cost Toews a chance to score 30 goals in 2016–17, but he reached the 20-goal mark for the 10th straight time by scoring twice against the Colorado Avalanche on March 19.

19. The 2013 Stanley Cup Final was one for the ages. Game 1 went into triple overtime before the Hawks won on a goal by Andrew Shaw after 52:08 of extra time. Boston won Game 2 in overtime at the United Center; the Blackhawks got even by winning Game 4 at Boston in overtime.

Chicago skated off with a 3–1 win in Game 5, giving the Hawks a 3–2 series lead and a chance to bring home the Stanley Cup for the third time in six seasons if they could win Game 6 at TD Bank Garden.

Boston's Chris Kelly scored the only goal of the first period. Jonathan Toews tied the game 1–1 early in the second. The teams traded chances until Milan Lucic beat Corey Crawford with 7:49 remaining in the third period to give Boston a 2–1 lead.

With time ticking down, it looked like the teams would be heading back to Chicago for a Game 7. But the Hawks had other ideas.

Dave Bolland was part of one of the best late-game comebacks in the history of the Stanley Cup Final.

Coach Joel Quenneville pulled Crawford in favor of an extra attacker. With the Hawks skating 6-on-5, Toews's pass from the left corner set up Bryan Bickell in the slot. His one-timer went through Boston goalie Tuukka Rask's five-hole. The resulting celebration was filled with as much relief as excitement.

But there was still 1:16 remaining before overtime, and the Hawks made it count.

With the Bruins still reeling, Dave Bolland beat Rask after Johnny Oduya's shot from the left point clanked off the left post. With 58.3 seconds remaining, the Hawks had gone from a one-goal deficit to a one-goal lead, thanks to the kind of rally that players and teams usually can only dream of.

"When don't you dream about it?" Bolland asked rhetorically after the 3–2 win. "We all dream about scoring that Stanley Cup winner."

Bolland had run through this exact moment in his mind as a kid playing hockey back home in Etobicoke, Ontario. He played on the street, on ponds, and at arenas across Southern Ontario region. Every once in a while he'd dream about scoring the Stanley Cup-winning goal.

"Check that one off the bucket list," Bolland said.

It was the second Cup for the Hawks under coach Joel Quenneville, and one that no one will ever forget.

"It's the greatest feeling in the world," he said. "Once you win one, you can't wait to do it again, but it's a hard road. We had some great hurdles, some great ups and downs here, but what a finish. I'm so happy for the guys."

"Amazing ending to an amazing year."

20. c. Denis Savard made 100-point seasons look easy. As a 20-year-old, he electrified Chicago with a 119-point season in

1981–82, then had 121 points the following season. In all, he exceeded 100 points five times in a span of seven seasons.

But aside from Savard, 100-point seasons have been kind of rare around the "Madhouse on Madison." Bobby Hull had no trouble reaching the 50-goal mark, but only in 1968–69 was he able to get to 100 points. His 107 points (58 goals, 49 assists) were the most he had in any season during his NHL career.

That's one more 100-point season than Stan Mikita had during his Hall of Fame career. Winning the Art Ross Trophy as the NHL's top scorer was one thing, but for all his scoring titles, Mikita never reached 100 points in a single season (though to be fair, his best offensive years came during the time when an NHL season was 70 games long).

Patrick Kane is on track for a career that will end with induction in the Hockey Hall of Fame, but his 106-point season in 2015–16 is still the only time he's exceeded 100 points.

No, the only other Blackhawk to break 100 points more than once was Jeremy Roenick, whose early-career offense was a big reason the Hawks were one of the NHL's top teams in the early seasons of the 1990s and even managed to get to the Stanley Cup Final in 1992.

After putting up 66 and 94 points in his first two full NHL seasons, Roenick had a breakout season in 1991–92, scoring 53 goals and adding 50 assists for 103 points, the most by a Hawk since Savard set the Blackhawks record with 131 in 1987–88.

He did even better in 1992–93, finishing with 50 goals and 57 points for 107 points, and matched that total in 1993–94 with 46 goals and 61 assists. Roenick played until 2008–09 but never came close to those numbers again.

Kane is the Hawks' lone 100-point scorer since Roenick's third and final season in triple figures.

21. b. For more than a decade, no one scored goals the way Bobby Hull did. In an era when players were much smaller and not nearly as strong as they are today, Hull stood out for his physical prowess, his speed, and his booming shot—which persuaded more than one NHL goaltender that wearing a facemask was a good idea.

Hull got his first NHL hat trick on December 6, 1959, when he scored three goals against the Boston Bruins at Boston Garden. It was the first of three hat tricks for Hull in the same month; he scored three times against the Toronto Maple Leafs at Chicago Stadium on December 20 and had three against the Bruins at the Stadium a week later.

Hull had his first four-goal game in the NHL against Toronto at Chicago Stadium on February 21, 1960.

From the time of his first hat trick until he left the Hawks following the 1971–72 season, Hull had at least one hat trick in every season except 1969–70, when he missed nine games and had "only" 38 goals.

Hull rebounded in 1970–71, finishing the season with three hat tricks; two of them came in a span of 15 days in February.

The Bruins and Maple Leafs continued to be his favorite victims when it came to hat tricks—he had seven against each of them. Hull also had five hat tricks against the New York Rangers, three against the Detroit Red Wings, two each against the California Golden Seals and Los Angeles Kings, and one each against the Minnesota North Stars and Pittsburgh Penguins.

Hull had 18 of his hat tricks in front of his home fans at Chicago Stadium. Of the 10 he had on the road, two each came in Boston, Toronto, and New York, with one apiece in Los Angeles, California, Detroit, and Pittsburgh. The last hat trick came on December 22, 1971, when Hull scored three goals against California at the Oakland Coliseum Arena.

His 28 hat tricks (24 three-goal games and four four-goal games) were the most in NHL history through the 1971–72 season. Today, Hull is tied for sixth in NHL history with Marcel Dionne; one of the five men ahead of him is his son, Brett Hull, who had 33.

22. a. Penalty shots by the Hawks in the Stanley Cup Playoffs have been few and far between. In fact, Chicago has had just five since entering the NHL in the 1926–27 season.

The first Chicago player to be awarded a penalty shot was Virgil Johnson, a US-born defenseman who became the first player in NHL history to receive a penalty shot in the Stanley Cup Final. It came in Game 4 of the 1944 Stanley Cup Final, but Johnson was unable to beat Montreal Canadiens goaltender Bill Durnan. The Canadiens won the game 5–4 in overtime to sweep the series.

No Hawk was awarded a penalty shot again until April 20, 1979, when forward Mike Walton received one with 1:42 remaining in the second period of Game 3 in their Quarterfinal series against the New York Islanders after defenseman Dave Lewis was called for covering the puck in the crease. Coach Bob Pulford could pick anyone on the ice to take the shot and chose Walton, who skated in but was denied by the pad of New York goaltender Glenn "Chico" Resch. The Islanders won the game 4–0.

The third Hawk to take a penalty shot in a playoff game was Patrick Poulin, who got the chance on May 9, 1995, against Toronto Maple Leafs goaltender Felix Potvin. Poulin didn't score and neither did the Blackhawks, who lost 3–0.

Michael Frolik became the first Blackhawk to score on a penalty shot during a Stanley Cup Playoff game when he beat Vancouver Canucks goaltender Cory Schneider at the United Center in Game 6 of their first-round series on April 24, 2011. Frolik raced in and beat Schneider, who was injured on the play and had to come out of the game. The goal tied the score 3–3, and the Hawks won 4–3 in overtime to even the series at 3–3 after losing the first three games, However, the Canucks won Game 7 to capture the series.

Michael Frolik has scored on two penalty shots in the Stanley Cup Playoffs.

Frolik made playoff history when he scored against Jimmy Howard of the Detroit Red Wings in Game 6 of the Western Conference First Round on May 27, 2013. Frolik became the first player in NHL history to score two penalty-shot goals in the playoffs.

"It's special to be first," he told the media afterward. "I was surprised no one did that before. For sure, it felt nice."

Frolik's perfect backhander into the top of the net proved to be the game-winning goal as the Hawks evened the series at 3–3, setting the stage for a Game 7 win in overtime.

23. d. The United Center is a great place to be a Blackhawk, and in the case of goaltender Corey Crawford during the 2015–16 season, when he played at home he was a good bet to get a shutout.

All seven of Crawford's shutouts in 2015–16 came at the United Center.

The first two came in consecutive games, and each required a little extra work. Crawford made 21 saves against the Tampa Bay Lightning on October 24 in a 1–0 shutout, with Jonathan Toews scoring the only goal of the game 17 seconds into overtime.

Two nights later, Crawford had to work a lot harder, stopping all 39 shots by the Anaheim Ducks before Toews came through again, this time 51 seconds into overtime, for another 1–0 win.

Crawford's next two shutouts also came in back-to-back games. He made 25 saves in a 2–0 victory against the Winnipeg Jets on December 11 (amazingly, Toews again had the winning goal), and stopped all 30 shots by the Vancouver Canucks in a 4–0 win on December 13 (Duncan Keith had the winning goal in that game).

Those two wins came at the start of a four-game home-stand. After a 3–0 loss to the Colorado Avalanche on December 15, Crawford was perfect once again two nights later in a 4–0 victory against the Edmonton Oilers. He made 33 saves, and for the fourth time in his five shutouts, Toews had the winning goal.

Crawford celebrated the new year with his sixth shutout, making 26 saves in a 3–0 victory against the Ottawa Senators on January 3. Toews didn't score, but Keith did—getting his second game-winner in a Crawford shutout.

The final shutout came exactly three weeks later against Chicago's Central Division rivals, the St. Louis Blues. In a tight-checking game that saw each team limited to 25 shots on goal, Crawford and the Hawks won 2–0. Artemi Panarin opened the scoring late in the second period, and Andrew Shaw gave Crawford some breathing room early in the third.

24. b. When the Blackhawks acquired forward Andrew Ladd on February 26, 2008, in a trade that sent forward Tuomo Ruutu to the Carolina Hurricanes, they hadn't won the Stanley Cup since 1961—but Ladd was less than two years removed from winning one. Ladd, the fourth player chosen in the 2004 NHL Draft, was a rookie with the Hurricanes in 2005–06, playing 29 regular-season games and finishing with 11 points (six goals, five assists).

That might not sound like a lot, but it was enough to earn Ladd a spot on Carolina's playoff roster, and he contributed five points (two goals, three assists) while serving as a useful role player on the franchise's first Stanley Cup team since joining the NHL as the Hartford Whalers in 1979.

Andrew Ladd was part of the 2010 Cup-winning team in his first stint with the Hawks.

Ladd continued to be used in more of a support role by the Hurricanes (he averaged less than 12 minutes of ice time per game) before being sent to the Blackhawks.

With more ice time in Chicago (an average of about 14 minutes a game), Ladd showed a lot more scoring touch than he had in Carolina. He had 12 points (five goals, seven assists) in 20 games with the Hawks after the trade, then finished with a career-high 49 points (15 goals, 34 assists) in 2008–09 and scored 17 goals in 2009–10.

Ladd also had three goals and three assists in 19 games to help the Hawks win their first Cup in 49 years—but his second in five seasons.

However, the salary cap forced the Blackhawks to deal Ladd during the summer of 2010. He went to the Atlanta Thrashers and wound up in a top-six role for the first time in his career, finishing with 29 goals and 59 points, though Atlanta missed the Stanley Cup Playoffs.

Ladd moved with the franchise to Winnipeg, was named captain, and became a reliable scorer for the Jets until the Hawks reacquired him for the stretch run in 2015–16. This trade didn't work out as well; although Ladd had eight goals and 12 points in 19 games in his second stint with the Hawks, the St. Louis Blues ended their hopes of repeating by outlasting Chicago in seven games in their Western Conference First Round series.

Once again, the salary cap made it impossible for the Blackhawks to keep Ladd; this time, he signed with the New York Islanders on July 1, 2016.

25. b. With offense in short supply these days, it's tempting to overlook Patrick Kane's NHL-best 106 points in 2015–16 when discussing the great seasons in franchise history. But in a league where the average game featured about 5.4 goals per game (about one-third less than the offensive bacchanalia of the early and mid-1980s), Kane's season was at least the equal of any in the past 50 years.

Kane was the biggest reason the Hawks' power play ranked second in the NHL (22.6 percent) and was third with

57 man-advantage goals scored. He scored 17 times with the extra man, not only surpassing his previous career high of 13 in 2008–09 but finishing with more than twice as many as runner-up Artemi Panarin, his linemate, who had eight.

When it came to game-winning goals, Kane again topped the Hawks—he had nine, one more than Jonathan Toews and two more than Panarin.

Nobody on the Hawks was close to Kane when it came to shots on goal. He finished the season with 287; that was 96 more than runner-up Marian Hossa. But it's not like he was shooting for the sake of shooting: Kane scored on 16.0 percent of his shots, matching Panarin, who took 187 shots. Among players who saw action in at least 30 games with Chicago, Kane was tied with Panarin in shooting percentage, trailing only the third member of their line, center Artem Anisimov (16.5 percent).

The one category in which Kane didn't lead the Hawks was shorthanded goals. Chicago finished in a four-way tie for third in the NHL with 10 shorthanded goals scored, but Kane didn't have any of them. In fact, he's never scored a shorthanded goal in his NHL career.

26. b. Patrick Kane was a deserving winner of the Hart Trophy as the NHL's most valuable player in 2015–16. He was also the first Hawk to win the award in almost 50 years.

It took nearly two decades from the time Chicago entered the NHL in 1926 for a Hawk to be recognized with the Hart Trophy. The first winner was Max Bentley, half of one of the best brother combinations of all time. Max and Doug Bentley had returned from World War II (Max missed two seasons, Doug missed one) and picked up where they had left off in terms of making life miserable for opposing goaltenders. Max led the NHL with 61 points (31 goals, 30 assists) in 1945–46 and was recognized as the league's MVP.

The Hawks had hit the skids by the time the 1953–54 season rolled around. They were in the midst of a 14-season stretch in which they failed to finish with a winning record, and after making the Stanley Cup Playoffs in 1952–53 (going 27–28–15), they collapsed in 1953–54, going 12–51–7 for 31 points, a distant last in the six-team NHL. Despite that, goaltender Al Rollins was voted as winner of the Hart Trophy.

Few goaltenders faced the barrage of attackers that Rollins saw in 1953–54. Given that Rollins played for a team that earned 31 of a possible 140 points, his 3.23 goals-against average (save percentage stats were still nearly three decades away) was pretty good considering he wasn't getting much help, and five of his 12 wins were shutouts. Rollins was the main reason a bad season wasn't worse.

The Blackhawks claimed the Hart Trophy for four consecutive seasons in the 1960s, with two Chicago legends winning twice each.

Bobby Hull won the Hart in 1964–65 after scoring 39 goals and finishing with 71 points in 61 games. He was second in the NHL in goals (though first in goals per game at 0.64) and finished fourth in points. Hull also won the Lady Byng Trophy, given for skillful and gentlemanly play.

If there was any question about whether Hull was the MVP in 1964–65, there was none in 1965–66, when he set an NHL single-season record for goals (54; runner-up Frank Mahovlich scored 32, one more than Hull's total of even-strength goals) and led the league with 97 points (teammate Stan Mikita and Montreal's Bobby Rousseau were tied for second with 78). Not surprisingly, the Hawks led the NHL in scoring with 240 goals in 70 games.

Hull led the NHL in goals in 1966–67 with 52, but Mikita went home with the Hart Trophy by piling up 97 points, including an NHL-leading 62 assists. Mikita's 35 goals were second to Hull, and Hull's 80 points were second to Mikita. Perhaps most amazing is that the two usually played on different lines and were rarely on the ice together. The Hawks finished first in the final season of the Original Six era, and their 264 goals were 52 more than the second-place Detroit Red Wings.

Mikita led the NHL in points again in 1967–68, finishing with 87 (an NHL career-high 40 goals, 47 assists), three more than former teammate Phil Esposito, who had been traded to the Boston Bruins. That was enough to make him the Hawks' second straight back-to-back Hart Trophy winner.

Little did anyone know it would take 48 years for another Blackhawk to win the Hart.

27. The Hawks have had a variety of players wear the captain's "C" since entering the NHL in 1926. The list begins with Dick Irvin, who served as captain for the franchise's first three seasons in the NHL, and runs to the current captain, Jonathan Toews. The Hawks have also gone without an official captain; it happened in 1950–51 and again from 1970–71 through 1974–75.

The list includes Charlie Gardiner, the only goaltender to have his name engraved on the Stanley Cup as a team captain. Gardiner was named captain for the 1933–34 season and led the Hawks to the first Stanley Cup in their history. Sadly, he didn't get an opportunity to go for a repeat. A few months after winning the Cup, Gardiner died from a brain hemorrhage. He was twenty-nine.

Johnny Gottselig succeeded Gardiner and served as captain for five years, including the Stanley Cup-winning season of 1938. Gottselig was the longest-serving Hawks captain through 1961, when Ed Litzenberger wore the "C" for Chicago's third Cup-winning team.

However, Litzenberger was lost in the intraleague draft a few months later, and defenseman Pierre Pilote assumed the captaincy. Pilote, a star defenseman, wore the "C" for seven seasons, the most in franchise history to that point, before being traded to the Toronto Maple Leafs in 1968.

No one matched Pilote's mark until Dirk Graham was named captain in 1988. Graham, a hard-working, two-way forward, matched Pilote's mark of seven seasons; he gave up the "C" after the 1994–95 season, when he retired.

The Hawks had six players serve as captain in the next 13 years (Martin Lapointe wore the "C" in the latter part of the 2005–06 season while Adrian Aucoin was injured) before Toews was named to the captaincy on July 18, 2008. At 20 years and 79 days, Toews was the youngest captain in the history of the Hawks and the third-youngest in NHL history.

Toews will enter his franchise-record 10th season as captain in 2017–18. He's also the only player in Hawks history to serve as captain of multiple Stanley Cup-winning teams.

28. a. Few teams have had as many as three players who've scored 400 or more goals (the New York Rangers, who entered the league along with the Hawks, have one, the same number as the Toronto Maple Leafs, who came into the NHL as the Toronto Arenas when the league formed in 1917).

The Blackhawks have been fortunate enough to have three, two of whom have been inducted into the Hockey Hall of Fame.

Bobby Hull and Stan Mikita (in any order you choose) are arguably the two best players in franchise history. Hull scored 604 goals with the Blackhawks and was coming off another 50-goal season in 1971–72 when he opted to become the first NHL star to sign with the new World Hockey Association.

Hull also scored 303 goals in 411 games during seven seasons with the WHA's Winnipeg Jets; it's hard to imagine that he wouldn't have surpassed Gordie Howe's NHL career record of 801 goals if he'd stayed in Chicago. He did get six more NHL goals with the Jets and Hartford Whalers in 1979–80 before retiring.

Mikita was more of a playmaker than a shooter, but he finished his 22 seasons in the NHL with 541 goals (and 926 assists). Mikita's biggest goal-scoring season was 1967–68, when he had 40, but he scored 20 or more goals in 14 consecutive seasons and had at least 16 goals in 19 consecutive seasons.

Though Denis Savard was among the NHL's greatest scorers of the 1980s and scored 32 or more goals in seven consecutive seasons, he was also more of a passer than a shooter. In 13 seasons with the Hawks (including two at the end of his career), Savard scored 377 goals but had 719 assists for 1,096 points in 881 games.

However, a lot of those assists went to the third player on the Hawks' 400-goal list. Steve Larmer spent much of his career playing right wing with Savard. Larmer never had 50 goals in a season, but he scored 41 or more five times and piled up 406 goals in 13 seasons with Chicago before ending up with the New York Rangers as part of a three-team trade on November 2, 1993.

29. Though the list is likely to grow in the near future, the Blackhawks ended the 2016–17 season with four players who've played 1,000 games in red, black, and white. But Stan Mikita has lapped the field.

Every one of Mikita's 1,394 NHL regular-season games was played with the Hawks. Mikita's first taste of the NHL came as an 18-year-old, when he played three games and had one assist in 1958–59. He became an NHL regular the following season and stayed that way through the 1960s and 1970s before playing 17 games in 1979–80, his final NHL season.

Bobby Hull might have come close to or even surpassed Mikita's total had he not signed with the Winnipeg Jets of the brand-new World Hockey Association in 1972. His career total of 1,036 games with Chicago was a franchise record until Mikita blew past it.

Eric Nesterenko was a contemporary of Hull and Mikita, but made his living as a rugged role player who could contribute some offense. Nesterenko spent his first four NHL seasons with the Toronto Maple Leafs before being acquired in a trade on May 21, 1956. Nesterenko surpassed the 1,000-game mark late in 1971–72, his final season with the Hawks, and ended his NHL career with 1,219 games played, 1,013 of them with the Hawks.

Bob Murray, the only defenseman on this list, spent all of his 15 NHL seasons with the Blackhawks before retiring after the 1989–90 season. Murray was Chicago's third-round pick (No. 52) in the 1974 NHL Draft. He made the Hawks as a 21-year-old in 1975–76 and scored as many as 19 goals

(1978–79) and finished with as many at 60 points (1980–81). Murray played 49 games in his final season, giving him 1,008 in his NHL career, all with the Hawks.

Two of Chicago's current stars figure to join the 1,000-game club in the near future. Brent Seabrook (923) and Duncan Keith (913), who've spent much of their careers as partners on the Hawks' blue line, figure to pass 1,000 games before long.

30. Once upon a time, analog scoreboard clocks were nothing unusual in NHL arenas. Boston Garden and the Detroit Olympia each had one, as did the pre-NHL Memorial Auditorium in Buffalo. But Detroit and Buffalo switched to digital timing in the mid-1960s, and Boston Garden's four-sided scoreboard was installed in time for the 1969–70 season, when the Bruins won the Stanley Cup.

Entering the 1970–71 season, Chicago Stadium was the last NHL arena to have a scoreboard with analog clocks. The "Sports Timer" scoreboard, built by Bulova and installed at the Stadium in 1943, featured a large 20-minute clock face that kept the time remaining in the period with a short, black minute hand and a longer red-colored second hand. There were also smaller clock faces to track penalty time; each of the five-minute penalty timers had its own single hand and clock face.

Many fans found it difficult to read how much time was left in a period on the main game timer's large face; each minute of play was marked by a longer line on every third "seconds" increment on the central main dial, due to the minute hand's 20-minute "full rotation" timing capacity for one period. For hockey, the only digital displays were for scoring and for the numbers of penalized players.

First Period

The Stadium finally got its own four-sided, digital-clock scoreboard; it was first used on September 21, 1975, for a preseason game. The new scoreboard, built by the Day Sign Company of Toronto, was much like the one that replaced an identical Bulova model at Boston Garden.

In 1985, the board was changed again, this time to one with a color electronic message board built by White Way Sign, which later built scoreboards for the United Center.

31. The Hawks have had a number of famous forward lines. The "Pony Line," featuring brothers Max Bentley and Doug Bentley along with Bill Mosienko, made life difficult for opposing goaltenders in the late 1940s (the name came from the fact that all three were on the small side size-wise). In the 1960s, the "Scooter Line," with Stan Mikita centering for Ken Wharram and Ab McDonald (later for Doug Mohns), was a threat to score every time they took the ice. And if dealing with those three wasn't tough enough, there was the "Million Dollar Line" of Bobby Hull, Bill Hay, and Murray Balfour (though as Hay was quick to point out to NHL.com in 2015, the name had nothing to do with what the threesome actually got paid). Hay and Balfour helped to make Hull one of the NHL's all-time leading scorers.

But the distinction of being the most productive trio in Hawks history belongs to "The Party Line," which had Denis Savard in the middle, Al Secord on the left, and rookie Steve Larmer on the right.

Secord and Savard were already established stars when Larmer burst into the NHL in 1982–83 and joined them to form one of the most feared trios of the 1980s. They combined for 297 points in 80 games, still the most of any line in Hawks history.

Savard, playing his third season, scored 35 goals and had 86 assists for 121 points, breaking the franchise single-season record he'd set in 1981–82. Secord, a power forward, had a career year with 54 goals and 86 points (plus 180 minutes in penalties).

Larmer, a sixth-round pick in the 1980 NHL Draft, proved to be a perfect complement. He finished his first full season with 90 points (43 goals, 47 assists) to win the Calder Trophy as the NHL's top rookie and kept piling up points even after his partners left.

32. The 1963–64 Hawks joined the 1944–45 Montreal Canadiens as the only teams to have five First-Team All-Stars. Each team had the same setup—the five All-Stars included a goaltender, one of the two defensemen, and all three forwards.

Glenn Hall had another superb season in goal for the Hawks. He led all NHL goaltenders with 34 victories, was third with a 2.30 goals-against average and second in shutouts with seven. Hall also tied for second in the NHL with 65 games played. Were the Vezina Trophy awarded under today's criteria, Hall would likely have won it.

Pierre Pilote tends to get overlooked when the discussion turns to great defensemen of the 1960s, but 1963–64 marked the second of five consecutive seasons in which he was a First-Team All-Star and the second of three straight in which he won the Norris Trophy. Pilote finished the season with 53 points (seven goals, 46 assists), easily tops among defensemen (no one else had more than 36). It was also his third season as captain. Pilote wasn't flashy, but he was oh-so-good.

The forwards were all Hawks.

Bobby Hull earned the nod on left wing after another typically brilliant season—a league-leading 43 goals and 87 points (two behind Mikita's 89). If there were a category for "goalies terrified," Hull would have led that one as well.

Mikita, the NHL scoring leader, earned First-Team honors at center for the third consecutive season. His 39 goals and 50 assists each tied him for second in the NHL; add them together and he earned his first of four scoring championships.

The right wing was Ken Wharram, who played with Mikita on the "Scooter Line." Wharram matched Mikita by finishing with career highs of 39 goals and 71 points. He and Mikita shared the NHL lead with 14 power-play goals each.

Together, Hull, Wharram, and Mikita combined for 121 of the Hawks' league-leading 218 goals.

The only non-Hawk on the First All-Star Team was defenseman Tim Horton, who helped the Toronto Maple Leafs win the Stanley Cup for the third consecutive year.

33. In a season that saw 177 shutouts around the league, it's hard to believe that the Blackhawks didn't have any in 2011–12.

Though the Blackhawks finished with a 45–26–11 record, good for 101 points in the power-packed Central Division, neither of their goaltenders, Corey Crawford and Ray Emery, were able to put up a zero.

It's not like they didn't have chances. The Blackhawks held the opposition to one goal 17 times (16 wins and a 1–0 loss to the San Jose Sharks on November 23, 2011). But overall, it was a tough defensive season for the Hawks, who finished 22nd in the NHL and 15th among the 16 playoff teams in goals allowed with 238.

More aggravating had to be the fact that the Hawks were shut out seven times, twice at the United Center and five times on the road.

Chicago didn't fare any better in the 2012 Stanley Cup Playoffs. The Hawks didn't have a shutout during their six-game series against the Phoenix (now Arizona) Coyotes, which ended at the United Center with a 4–0 loss.

Ironically, those numbers were exactly reversed one year later—Chicago shut out opponents seven times (two at home, five on the road) and was not shut out during the regular season.

34. a. Joel Quenneville's name doesn't come trippingly off the tongue when the discussion turns to the NHL's all-time coaching greats, but it should.

Quenneville took over on October 16, 2008, after the Blackhawks got off to a slow start under Denis Savard, and led them to the Western Conference Final. One year later, they completed the climb back to the top of the NHL by winning the Stanley Cup.

Perhaps amazingly, the Blackhawks have won more than half of their games in every season since Quenneville took over. They've never won fewer than 44 games (2010–11) in an 82-game season, went 36–7–5 during the abbreviated 48-game 2012–13 season, and won 50 games in 2016–17.

Quenneville's best full season was 2009–10, when the Blackhawks rolled to 52 wins and won the Central Division by 10 points. He's been a consistent winner in Chicago (as he was, for the most part, in Colorado and St. Louis), and is comfortably ensconced as the second-winningest coach in NHL history.

35. d. The Hawks have had a variety of farm teams since the practice of having minor league developmental clubs became popular among NHL teams.

Not surprisingly, in Chicago's case, many of their affiliates have been located in the Midwest. Before the Blues arrived in St. Louis in 1967, the Hawks had an affiliate there on three occasions. The last one, the St. Louis Braves, was a member of the Central Hockey League from 1963–67.

With the arrival of the Blues, the Hawks moved their primary affiliate to Dallas for the next 11 seasons. The CHL's Dallas Black Hawks saw dozens of future NHL players pass through; among the most notable was future Chicago captain Dirk Graham (62 games in 1979–80). Owing largely to their location, the Black Hawks and Fort Worth Wings/Texans were one of the best minor league rivalries.

Beginning in 1978–79, Chicago changed teams and leagues, putting its top prospects with the New Brunswick Hawks of the American Hockey League. Players such as defenseman Jack O'Callahan spent time in New Brunswick, but perhaps the most notable future Hawk to spend time with the team was coach Orval Tessier, who led New Brunswick to a Calder Cup championship in 1981–82, then moved on to Chicago.

After brief stints of using Springfield (AHL), Milwaukee (IHL), and Nova Scotia (AHL), the Blackhawks brought their prospects closer to home in 1987. The Saginaw Hawks lasted for two seasons, each of which featured future Hall of Famer Ed Belfour in goal.

The Blackhawks switched their affiliate to the Indianapolis Ice from 1989–98. After one season each in Portland (AHL) and Cleveland (IHL), the Hawks found a home for their prospects with the AHL's Norfolk Admirals from 2000–07.

But in 2007, the Hawks brought their prospects much closer to home. The city of Rockford, Illinois, purchased the former Cincinnati Mighty Ducks franchise from the AHL and it became the IceHogs.

Perhaps surprisingly, the Hawks have never been affiliated with the Chicago Wolves throughout that franchise's tenure in the IHL or AHL. The Wolves, who play in suburban Rosemont, Illinois, served as the top farm team of the Atlanta Thrashers and Vancouver Canucks and the St. Louis Blues before becoming the AHL affiliate of the new Vegas Golden Knights beginning in the 2017–18 season.

36. c. Corey Crawford was off to perhaps the best start of his NHL career in 2016–17 when the word came down just before the Blackhawks' game against the Philadelphia Flyers at Wells Fargo Center on December 3 that Crawford wasn't feeling well and would be a late scratch.

A couple of hours later, the Hawks disclosed that Crawford had undergone an appendectomy and would miss at least two weeks.

Crawford was 12–6–2 with a 2.27 goals-against average and .927 save percentage in 20 games.

"He's the best goalie in the League; him and [Montreal's] Carey Price, you can put them in a category by themselves," said Scott Darling, Crawford's backup, who wound up starting every game until his return. "He brings it every night. He's been great all year. And he's just a great guy. Just one of the boys. We missed him in the room for sure."

The most excited person that day was Eric Semborski, who was signed to an amateur tryout and served as Darling's backup. Semborski, 23, was a goaltender on the Temple University club hockey team who works as coach and instructor with the Ed Snider Youth Hockey Foundation in Philadelphia.

Crawford missed three weeks of action before returning.

37. a. Dick Redmond's NHL career took a big step forward on December 5, 1972, when the Hawks acquired him in a trade that sent Darryl Maggs to the California Golden Seals.

Redmond had shown flashes of potential with the Golden Seals after coming from the Minnesota North Stars in a trade, but he blossomed upon his arrival in Chicago. With Bobby Hull gone to the World Hockey Association, the Hawks were trying to keep their hold on the West Division, and the addition of Redmond gave Chicago an offensive boost on the blue line. He finished his first season in Chicago with 28 points (nine goals, 19 assists) in 52 games after the trade.

Redmond's first Stanley Cup Playoff game was one for the franchise record book. In the first game of their opening-round series against the St. Louis Blues, Redmond opened the scoring at 15:02 of the first period, then set a franchise record for the fastest two goals in a playoff game when he beat Wayne Stephenson just 18 seconds later, giving the Hawks a 2–0 lead.

Chicago still led 2–0 early in the second period when Redmond completed his hat trick at 2:13 of the second period. The Hawks kept rolling and finished with a 7–1 victory, starting them on the way to a five-game victory in which they outscored the Blues 22–9.

The three goals in a span of 7:11 are still the fastest three goals by any Blackhawk in a playoff game.

There was another franchise first in the game: Center Pit Martin scored Chicago's final three goals for a second (natural) hat trick, marking the first time two Hawks had scored three goals in the same game.

Redmond also became the first defenseman in franchise history to have a hat trick in a playoff game, an accomplishment not matched until Gary Suter scored three times in a game on April 24, 1994. He scored as many as 22 goals (1976–77) and had as many as 59 points (1973–74) during his five seasons in Chicago. The younger brother of 50-goal scorer Mickey Redmond finished his NHL career with 445 points (133 goals, 312 assists) in 771 NHL games. He also had nine goals in 66 Stanley Cup Playoff games—one-third of them in a sensational stretch during his first postseason game.

38. Bobby Hull couldn't do it. Neither could Stan Mikita, or Denis Savard, or Tony Amonte, or Jeremy Roenick. Only Doug Bentley and Pit Martin were able to score three goals in a playoff game twice in the same year.

The Blackhawks had never had a playoff hat trick until Bentley scored three times in a 7–1 victory against the Detroit Red Wings at Chicago Stadium on March 28, 1944. That win gave the Hawks a 3–1 lead in the series, and Bentley helped send the Wings home for the summer when he scored three more goals two nights later in a 5–2 series-clinching win in Detroit.

Through the next 29 years, just two Chicago players scored three times in a playoff game. Hull did it nearly nine years apart, at Detroit on April 7, 1963, and at Pittsburgh on April 9, 1972. Jim Pappin was the other; he scored three times at Philadelphia on April 11, 1971.

But in 1973, Pit Martin did it twice—amazingly, in the Hawks' first and last playoff games of the year.

Martin had a natural hat trick in the Hawks' playoff opener, a 7–1 victory against the St. Louis Blues at Chicago

Stadium on April 4, 1973. He did it again on May 10, 1973, becoming the first player in franchise history to score three times in a Stanley Cup Final game. Unfortunately for Martin and the Hawks, the three goals weren't enough; the Montreal Canadiens won 6–4 at Chicago Stadium in Game 6 to capture the Cup.

Since then, the only time the Blackhawks as a team have had two hat tricks in the same playoff year was in 1994. Tony Amonte had a four-goal night against the Toronto Maple Leafs in Game 3 of the Western Conference Quarterfinals on April 23, a 5–4 victory at Chicago Stadium. One night later, defenseman Gary Suter scored all three of the Hawks' goals in regulation before Roenick connected 1:23 into overtime for a 4–3 series-tying victory. Unfortunately, the Leafs won the next two games, each by a score of 1–0, and the series.

39. b. It took 1,240 regular-season games, but Marian Hossa scored his 500th NHL goal in the first full week of the 2016–17 season. He became the 44th player in league history to score 500 goals and the third from Slovakia (joining Hawks legend Stan Mikita and Peter Bondra, who scored most of his 503 goals with the Washington Capitals but got No. 500 as a Hawk).

Hossa shouted, "Yeah, baby!" after his backhander beat Philadelphia Flyers goaltender Michal Neuvirth for the milestone goal at 5:04 of the second period. It came after a typical Hossa power move to the net in which he shrugged off defenseman Andrew MacDonald before scoring the goal that put the Hawks up 4–0 and ended Neuvirth's night.

Hossa got a prolonged standing ovation and took a curtain call at center ice.

"To tell you the truth, it just felt great," Hossa said. "Great reception from the fans. It's 500 goals. I'm just glad to be a part of that company and thank all my teammates who I played with."

Hossa became the fifth player to score his 500th goal with the Blackhawks, tying the Detroit Red Wings for the most of any team. Bobby Hull was the first, on February 21, 1970, then Stan Mikita on February 27, 1977, Michel Goulet on February 16, 1992, and Bondra on December 22, 2006.

Hossa had been sitting on 499 goals for nearly seven months. No. 499 came on March 29, 2016, and he was expected to reach 500 before the end of the 2015–16 season. However, injuries and a big drop in his shooting percentage left Hossa with a career-low 13 goals and sent him home for the summer one goal shy of 500.

One thing that especially pleased Hossa was that he had to work for the goal.

"I definitely didn't want to take No. 500 into an empty net," he said.

The Flyers nearly spoiled the party, rallying from a four-goal deficit to tie the game before the Blackhawks regained control and went on to a 7–4 win.

40. c. The Montreal Canadiens have been the bane of the Hawks for much of their existence, especially at playoff time.

The Hawks have faced the Canadiens 17 times, more than any other opponent. But they've won just five of those series, only two in the past 75 years—and none in five tries in the Stanley Cup Final.

The first one came in 1931, when the Canadiens won Games 4 and 5 to take the best-of-five Final series. Chicago got within one game of its first championship with a 3–2 win in triple overtime of Game 3 at the Forum. But the Canadiens evened the series with a 4–2 win in Game 4, then took home the Cup by winning 2–0 in Game 5, with Johnny Gagnon and Howie Morenz scoring for the Canadiens.

The Hawks got a bit of revenge by defeating the Canadiens in the Quarterfinals in 1934 and again in 1938, then going on to win the Cup each time. They also defeated Montreal in the 1941 Quarterfinals.

The teams met again in the 1944 Final, when the powerful Canadiens rolled to a four-game sweep, outscoring the Hawks 16–8.

Montreal defeated Chicago in four consecutive Semifinal series (1946, 1953, 1959, and 1960), but the Hawks ended Montreal's quest for a sixth straight championship by upsetting the Canadiens in six games in the 1961 semis—and as had happened in 1934 and 1938, they went on to win the Cup.

Chicago got to the 1962 Final with another six-game series win against Montreal in the Semifinals and had a chance to make it three straight when they faced the Canadiens in the 1965 Final. But after the home team won each of the first six games, the Canadiens scored quickly in Game 7 and went on to a 4–0 win at the Forum.

Montreal won a five-game Semifinal series in 1968, but it's the 1971 Stanley Cup Final loss that still sticks in the craw of Hawks fans. Montreal started a rookie goaltender (Ken Dryden) and had upset the Boston Bruins in the opening round before defeating the Minnesota North Stars to get to the Final. As was the case six years earlier, the home team won each of the first six games. But this time, Game 7 was scheduled for Chicago Stadium.

The Hawks jumped out to a 2–0 lead, but Jacques Lemaire's slap shot from the red line beat Tony Esposito to give the Canadiens new life, and two goals by Henri Richard gave Montreal a stunning 3–2 victory.

The teams met again in the Final two years later, with the Canadiens winning a wild six-game series that featured Chicago's 8–7 win in Game 5, still the highest-scoring game in the history of the Final.

Montreal and Chicago haven't seen each other in the playoffs since 1976, when a powerhouse Canadiens team swept the Hawks, outscoring them 13–3. With the teams now in opposite conferences, the only way they'll face each other in the playoffs is in the Final.

OK. You've had some time to get a little rest, maybe grab some refreshments and collect a few words about what you can do better in the next 20 minutes. It's time to lace 'em up again and get ready for period No. 2.

Here we go . . .

1. The NHL's salary cap means that the teams like the Black-hawks have to find talent in some unconventional places. One of their best recent finds was left wing Artemi Panarin, who came to the Hawks as an almost-25-year-old rookie and had 30 goals and 77 points in his first NHL season, then had 31 goals and 74 points in 2016-17, earning Sec-ond-Team All-Star honors on left wing. Which was the last team Panarin played for prior to coming to Chicago? (Give yourself an extra point if you know the nickname he quickly picked up.) *Answer on page 71.*
   a) Ak Bars Kazan (KHL)
   b) SKA St. Petersburg (KHL)
   c) Jokerit (KHL)
   d) MoDo (Swedish Hockey League)

2. The Black Hawks/Blackhawks have always been a good home team, whether that home was Chicago Stadium or the United Center. But what was their best season playing in front of their home fans? *Answer on page 72.*

3. Joel Quenneville earned his 400th victory as coach of the Blackhawks during the 2016–17 season. He has long since

passed every Chicago coach—except one. Who is the only coach in franchise history to have more wins behind the Blackhawks' bench than "Q?" *Answer on page 74.*

4. The Blackhawks have been a regular participant in outdoor games during the past decade. Which of these venues has *not* hosted a game involving the Hawks? *Answer on page 75.*
a) Wrigley Field
b) Busch Stadium
c) Fenway Park
d) TCF Bank Stadium

5. In the nine decades the Blackhawks have been in the NHL, they've overcome a 3–1 deficit to win a playoff series just once. In what year did they win the last three games of a series to keep their Stanley Cup hopes alive? *Answer on page 78.*
a) 2013
b) 2010
c) 1973
d) 1961

6. The franchise single-season record-holders for power-play goals and shorthanded goals were teammates in the late 1980s and early 1990s. Who are they? *Answer on page 79.*

7. Some of the greatest goaltenders in NHL history have played for the Hawks. But only one of them has had 40 or more wins in a season. Who was he? *Answer on page 81.*
a) Glenn Hall
b) Ed Belfour
c) Tony Esposito
d) Corey Crawford

8. Only one Chicago player has scored five goals in a regular-season game. Who is he? *Answer on page 83.*

9. The Blackhawks have played in more than 110 Stanley Cup Playoff series since entering the NHL for the 1926–27 season. They've faced 22 of the other 29 current teams at least once. Which one have they defeated the most often? *Answer on page 84.*
a) Boston Bruins
b) Montreal Canadiens
c) Toronto Maple Leafs
d) Detroit Red Wings

10. In addition to the 22 current teams they've opposed in the playoffs, the Blackhawks (in their days as the Black Hawks) have played two series each against two teams that are no longer part of the NHL. Which teams are they, and how did the Hawks fare? *Answer on page 85.*

11. One reason for the Hawks' continued success has been the ability of general manager Stan Bowman to find replacements for players he's had to trade in order to stay under the salary cap. One of those players is center Artem Anisimov, who was acquired during the summer of 2015. From which team did the Blackhawks get Anisimov? *Answer on page 87.*
a) Boston Bruins
b) New York Rangers
c) Columbus Blue Jackets
d) Central Red Army (KHL)

12. Glenn Hall holds an NHL record that, it's pretty safe to say, will never be broken; he played in more consecutive games than any goaltender in NHL history. How long was his consecutive-games streak? *Answer on page 88.*

13. In 2015–16, Patrick Kane became the first Blackhawk in nearly 50 years (and the first US-born player ever) to win both the Art Ross Trophy (leading scorer) and the Hart Trophy (most valuable player). Who was the last Blackhawk to pull off that daily double before Kane did it? *Answer on page 89.*
a) Stan Mikita
b) Bobby Hull
c) Denis Savard
d) Jeremy Roenick

14. Jonathan Toews is the only Blackhawk who's a member of one of the most exclusive clubs in hockey—the Triple Gold Club. What did he have to accomplish to earn admission? *Answer on page 91.*

15. The Blackhawks have had a player score four or more goals in a game 30 times. How many players have done it more than once? *Answer on page 92.*
a) 2
b) 4
c) 6
d) 8

16. Who are the only brothers to coach the Blackhawks? *Answer on page 93.*

17. The Blackhawks and Toronto Maple Leafs played a "perfect game" at Chicago Stadium on February 20, 1944. What made it perfect? *Answer on page 95.*
a) Blackhawks won 10–0
b) Blackhawks won 8–0 and won all three fights
c) Neither team scored or took a penalty
d) Neither team scored, Blackhawks won three fights

18. The Blackhawks hosted the 1991 NHL All-Star Game, which the Campbell Conference won 11–5. But the most memorable moment of the game had nothing to do with what happened on the ice. What was it? *Answer on page 95.*

19. May 15, 1967, is a day all Chicago hockey fans rue. That was the day the Hawks made a trade they'd much rather forget. Which team made the trade with Chicago, and who were the players involved? *Answer on page 97.*

20. Which of these expansion teams did not play its first NHL game against the Blackhawks? *Answer on page 98.*
a) Edmonton Oilers
b) Florida Panthers
c) Tampa Bay Lightning
d) San Jose Sharks

21. The Blackhawks are perfect against one NHL team in the 2010 decade (meaning they've won every game; no overtime or shootout losses), through the 2016–17 season. Which team is it, and how many games have they won? *Answer on page 100.*

22. The run to the Stanley Cup in 2015 featured the longest game in franchise history. Who was the opponent and how did the game end? *Answer on page 101.*

23. Steve Larmer was one of the Hawks' most reliable scorers for much of the 1980s and into the 1990s. What NHL record did he set? *Answer on page 103.*
a) Most goals by a right wing with one team
b) Most consecutive games played with one team
c) Most points by a rookie right wing
d) Most assists by a rookie

24. Joel Quenneville has coached the Blackhawks to more Stanley Cup championships than anyone in franchise history. But before he went into coaching, Quenneville was a defenseman who played more than 800 NHL games. Which of these teams did he NOT play for? *Answer on page 104.*
a) Colorado Rockies
b) Toronto Maple Leafs
c) Chicago Blackhawks
d) New Jersey Devils

25. Only one member of the Blackhawks has had more than 360 shots on goal in a season—and he did it three times. Who was he? *Answer on page 106.*

26. Who was the last man to serve as coach and general manager of the Blackhawks? *Answer on page 107.*
a) Mike Keenan
b) Tommy Ivan
c) Bob Pulford
d) Scotty Bowman

27. 2016–17 was Joel Quenneville's ninth season as coach of the Blackhawks. How many times have they missed the Stanley Cup Playoffs with "Q" behind the bench? *Answer on page 109.*
a) 0
b) 1
c) 2
d) 3

28. Defenseman Brian Campbell returned to the Blackhawks in 2016–17 for a second stint in Chicago. In which year was Campbell originally drafted, and by what team? *Answer on page 110.*

29. Corey Crawford has shared the William Jennings Trophy, given to the goalies on the team who allow the fewest regular-season goals, on two occasions—once with his partner in Chicago and the other with a goalie from another team. Who were the players he shared the award with, and in what years did it happen? *Answer on page 111.*

30. As of the end of the 2016–17 season, how long had Jonathan Toews been captain of the Blackhawks? *Answer on page 113.*
a) 7 seasons
b) 8 seasons
c) 9 seasons
d) 10 seasons

31. Which of these team records does Jeremy Roenick NOT hold? *Answer on page 114.*
a) Most game-winning goals in one season
b) Most shorthanded goals in one season
c) Most power-play goals in one season
d) Most goals by a center in one season

32. How many times did Bobby Hull lead the NHL in goals? *Answer on page 115.*
a) 5
b) 6
c) 7
d) 8

33. When goaltender Glenn Hall left the Blackhawks, where did he go? *Answer on page 117.*
a) Detroit Red Wings
b) Montreal Canadiens

c) Minnesota North Stars
d) St. Louis Blues

34. Who was the first Blackhawk to lead the NHL in scoring? *Answer on page 118.*
a) Max Bentley
b) Doug Bentley
c) Bill Mosienko
d) Bobby Hull

35. The Blackhawks have had 11 100-point seasons in their history. How many players combined to produce those 11 seasons, and who are they? *Answer on page 120.*

36. Who holds the Blackhawks' record for most penalty minutes in a season? *Answer on page 122.*
a) Wayne Van Dorp
b) Dave Manson
c) Bob Probert
d) Mike Peluso

37. One member of the Blackhawks put on a sharpshooting exhibition against the Vancouver Canucks on February 5, 1995. Not only did he score four goals, but he did it by taking just four shots on goal. Who was he? *Answer on page 123.*
a) Jeremy Roenick
b) Bernie Nicholls
c) Eric Daze
d) Brian Noonan

38. Having a player get a hat trick is tough enough, but having two players get one in the same game is almost impossible. However, it does happen. How many times have the

Blackhawks had two players score three or more goals in a game, and who were the players involved? *Answer on page 124.*

39. When the Blackhawks defeated the Los Angeles Kings 3–0 at the United Center on October 30, 2016, it was the 250th regular-season home shutout in franchise history. The Hawks have hit double digits in home shutouts just once since entering the NHL in 1926. When did it happen, and how many shutouts did they have? *Answer on page 126.*

40. The adoption of the shootout for the 2005–06 season meant there would be no more scoreless ties (if a game is scoreless through the regulation 60 minutes and five minutes of overtime, it's decided in the penalty-shot tiebreaker, though the two goaltenders each receive credit for a shutout). When did the Blackhawks play their last 0–0 tie, who was the opponent, and which Chicago goaltender pitched the 65-minute shutout? (Hint: Several years later, this goaltender figured in one of the great moments in Hawks history.) *Answer on page 127.*

There's the horn . . . the second period is in the books. Time to tromp back to the locker room, get some hydration, listen to a few well-chosen words from the coaching staff, and prepare to come out ready for the third period.

SECOND
PERIOD—ANSWERS

1. b. The salary cap, which became part of the NHL in the Collective Bargaining Agreement that settled a lockout in 2005, is designed to help lower-revenue teams keep up with their big-money brethren. It presents a challenge to successful teams, who have to figure out which players to lock up with long-term contracts and which can be replaced with lower-priced talent.

The Blackhawks have been among the NHL's best (and smartest) at finding ways to keep their nucleus intact while filling in with younger players and undervalued vets. It means that GM Stan Bowman and his staff have to leave no stone unturned.

That's how Artemi Panarin came to be a Blackhawk.

Panarin's maternal grandfather had played amateur hockey and encouraged him from a very young age to play. He was part of the Russian team that won gold at the 2011 IIHF World Junior Championship and scored the game-winning goal against Canada in the championship. That was after he had gone undrafted by all 30 NHL teams in 2010. Instead, he joined Vilyaz Chekhov of the Kontinental Hockey League, the top league in Russia. He spent part of the 2011–12 season with Ak Bars Kazan, returned to Vilyaz Chekhov for most of the 2012–13, and was acquired by SKA St. Petersburg in time to play three regular-season games.

Panarin broke out with 20 goals and 40 points for SKA St. Petersburg in 2013–14, then brought his game to another level in 2014–15 with 26 goals and 62 points in 54 games, earning First-Team All-Star honors. He also had five goals and 15 assists in 20 playoff games, helping his team win the Gagarin Cup (the KHL's version of the Stanley Cup).

After also excelling at the IIHF World Championship and helping Russia win the silver medal, Panarin was courted by a number of NHL teams (he was a free agent because he'd never been drafted). The Blackhawks, coming off their third Stanley Cup in a span of six seasons, knew they wouldn't be able to keep young star Brandon Saad (who ended up being traded), and saw Panarin as a way to replace him.

Chicago signed Panarin on April 29, 2015. He scored against future Hall of Fame goaltender Henrik Lundqvist in his NHL debut and found instant chemistry with Patrick Kane and fellow Russian Artem Anisimov. He also quickly picked up a nickname—"The Bread Man"—because his last name sounded like the name of the popular restaurant chain (Panera Bread).

Panarin finished his first NHL season with 30 goals and 47 assists for 77 points, earning the Calder Trophy as the league's top rookie, then went 31-43-74 in his second season. Panarin signed a two-year contract extension worth plenty of "bread"—$12 million over two seasons—but was sent to the Columbus Blue Jackets on June 23, 2017, in a trade that brought Saad back to Chicago.

2. Chicago has always been a wonderful place to play—as long as you're wearing a Hawks uniform. They broke the 20-win mark at home for the first time in 1960–61, when a 20–6–9 record at Chicago Stadium helped them finish third and earn the chance to bring back the Stanley Cup for the first time since 1938.

The Hawks won 20 or more home games every season from 1962–63 through 1969–70, going 24–5–6 in 35 games in 1966–67 (when they finished first in the regular season for the first time) and 26–7–5 in 1969–70, when the arrival of Tony Esposito made life miserable for opposing shooters.

But the next two seasons were all-timers.

The Black Hawks set a franchise record for home victories in 1970–71 by going 30–6–3—still the only 30-win home season in franchise history. Chicago went 16–0–2 in its first 18 games at the Stadium that season before losing 4–2 to the Los Angeles Kings on January 6, 1971. They were 30–4–3 until losing to the Montreal Canadiens and Toronto Maple Leafs on the final two Sundays of the season.

The Hawks outscored their opponents 153–78, allowing an average of two goals per game in their 39 home games.

There weren't as many victories in the following season, 1971–72, but Chicago's 28–3–8 record actually produced one more point (64–63). The Hawks won their first nine games at Chicago Stadium and were 15–0–2 through 17 games before the Boston Bruins came to town on December 29, 1971, and left with a 5–1 victory.

The good times resumed after that blip. Chicago went 9–0–3 in its next 12 home games before the Bruins returned on February 20, 1972, and won 3–1. The Buffalo Sabres arrived three nights later and escaped with a 2–1 win thanks to third-period goals by Craig Ramsay and Gerry Meehan, and 30 saves by Dave Dryden (Ken's big brother).

But those were the only losing nights at home during the season. Chicago closed the regular season at home with four wins and three ties. For the season, the Hawks scored 139 goals in 39 home games and allowed just 63.

There have been other excellent seasons; the Hawks went 29–8–3 in 40 games during the 1982–83 season, 28–8–4 in 1990–91, and 29–8 with four overtime/shootout losses in 2009–10. But the back-to-back seasons of 1970–71 and 1971–72 have yet to be duplicated.

3. You can argue that Joel Quenneville is the best coach in franchise history (and few if any Hawks fans would argue against someone who's brought three championships in a span of six seasons). But it will take a few more years for Quenneville to catch up to the franchise record for regular-season wins.

Billy Reay led the Hawks to the Stanley Cup Playoffs 12 times in 14 seasons.

That record belongs to Billy Reay, who was behind the bench from 1963–77 and piled up 516 victories in his 14 seasons, 12 of which ended with a trip to the Stanley Cup Playoffs. The only drawback was that none of them ended with a Stanley Cup championship.

Reay did get the Hawks to the Final twice, but they lost to the Montreal Canadiens in seven games in 1971 and in six games two years later.

Still, Reay finished his time in Chicago with a 516-335-161 record and a .589 point percentage (better than everyone except Quenneville, although in Reay's era, games that were tied after 60 minutes ended that way).

Reay's 1,012 games coached are also a franchise record and will remain so for at least another four years. If Quenneville stays behind the Hawks' bench, he'll pass that mark late in the 2020–21 season.

Reay and Quenneville have lapped the field a few times in both wins and games coached. Bob Pulford, who had four stints as the bench boss, is a distant third with 426 games coached and 182 victories.

4. c. The Blackhawks haven't been involved in every NHL outdoor game. It only seems that way.

In fact, they didn't take it outdoors until New Year's Day 2009, when the Detroit Red Wings came to Wrigley Field for the second edition of the NHL's Winter Classic. The 40,818 fans who packed the Friendly Confines saw the Hawks race out to a 3–1 lead after the first period only to allow five consecutive goals and lose 6–4 to the defending Stanley Cup champions.

The Blackhawks wore sweaters that were a mix of their 1936–37 and 1937–38 editions, with the design from 1936–37 and the crest on the chest from 1937–38. Cubs Hall of Famers Billy Williams, Ferguson Jenkins, and Ryne Sandberg were part of the pregame ceremonies, as were a number of retired Blackhawks. The teams changed sides midway though the third to equalize the weather conditions. During the break, Sandberg joined Bobby Hull, Stan Mikita, and Denis Savard in singing a hockey-flavored variation of "Take Me Out to the Ball Game."

By the time the Blackhawks went back outdoors, they were the defending Stanley Cup champions. That game took place on March 1, 2014, when the Hawks welcomed the Pittsburgh Penguins to Soldier Field as part of the NHL's Stadium Series. The game was played during a steady snowfall that forced the teams to simplify their style of play and kept the shoveling crew busy all night.

Playing a simple style worked perfectly for the Hawks, who rolled to a 5–1 victory. Jonathan Toews scored twice and had an assist, and Chicago stifled Pittsburgh star Sidney Crosby.

"I think we kept it really simple early on in the game and just threw pucks on the ice and chased after them," Toews said. "Nice shot by [Patrick Sharp] to get it started and we weren't sure how many more goals we were going to get after that . . . it was kind of come and go as far as the ice conditions."

The snow might have slowed down the players, but it didn't keep 62,921 fans from cheering on the Hawks at the home of the Chicago Bears. The game was also a hit with television viewers around the nation. It was played in prime time on NBC, and it produced a 2.1 national rating, the highest rating for a regular-season game outside the Winter Classic since NBC took over the broadcast contract.

By now, the Hawks were becoming an annual fixture outdoors. They were back at the Winter Classic in 2015, this time as the visiting team against the Washington Capitals at Nationals Park in the nation's capital.

This time, the Hawks wore jerseys based on their 1957 model—white with red and black striping on the bottom, lace-up collars, and the tomahawk logo near the elbows. They looked terrific but ended up going home disappointed when ex-Hawk Troy Brouwer scored a power-play goal with 13 seconds remaining in regulation time to give Washington a 3–2 victory. Sharp and Brandon Saad scored for Chicago, which overcame an early 2–0 deficit.

Seeing the Hawks play outdoors once a year was getting to be an annual rite of winter. Unfortunately for Chicago fans, their appearance in the 2016 NHL Stadium Series game against the Minnesota Wild at TCF Bank Stadium in Minneapolis on February 21 turned out to be a clunker.

The Wild scored two goals in each period and cruised to a 6–1 victory. Patrick Kane enabled the Hawks to avoid being shut out by scoring his 35th goal of the season at 12:05 of the third period. Chicago actually had a good number of scoring chances but could get only one shot past Wild goaltender Devan Dubnyk.

For 2017, the Blackhawks were back in the Winter Classic, this time against another Central Division rival, the St. Louis Blues, at Busch Stadium on January 2. First-year defenseman Michal Kempny gave the Blackhawks a 1–0 lead 62 seconds into the game, but Patrik Berglund tied the game in the second period and Vladimir Tarasenko scored twice in the third period to help St. Louis to a 4–1 win.

The Hawks still haven't made a trip to Fenway Park, but you never know.

5. a. Going down 3–1 in a playoff series is usually a quick ticket to the golf course, and the Blackhawks are no exception. For more than 8½ decades, the Hawks lost every best-of-seven series in which they dropped three of the first four games.

Hence, the odds didn't look good when the Blackhawks lost Games 2, 3, and 4 of their 2013 Western Conference Semifinal series to the Detroit Red Wings after a 4–1 win in Game 1. Chicago managed just two goals in the three losses and didn't score at all in a 2–0 loss in Game 4 at Joe Louis Arena.

But rather than fold up their tent, the Blackhawks got to work.

Andrew Shaw and Jonathan Toews scored power-play goals late in the second period and Shaw scored again in the third to give the Hawks a 4–1 win at the United Center in Game 5. Corey Crawford made 25 saves.

But things didn't look good after the second period of Game 6. Chicago took an early lead on Marian Hossa's power-play goal, but the Red Wings tied the game on a goal by Patrick Eaves and went ahead when Joakim Andersson beat Crawford midway through the second period.

However, the Hawks got even 51 seconds into the third period on a goal by Michal Handzus and regained the lead at 5:48 when Bryan Bickell scored. Michael Frolik made it 4–2 when he scored on a penalty shot at 9:43, and that proved to be the game-winner when Detroit's Damian Brunner beat Crawford with 52 seconds remaining.

That brought the series back to the United Center, and the Hawks delighted their fans when Patrick Sharp opened the scoring 1:08 into the second period. Chicago took its 1–0 lead into the dressing room at the second intermission, only to have Detroit's Henrik Zetterberg tie the game 26 seconds into the third period.

The Blackhawks thought they had gone ahead with less than two minutes remaining in regulation. However, Andrew Shaw's apparent goal was waved off by referee Stephen Walkom, who called a pair of minor penalties behind the play.

Instead, the game went into overtime, and defenseman Brent Seabrook got the chance to play hero.

Seabrook picked up a loose puck and skated in on goaltender Jimmy Howard through the middle of the ice, with Detroit defenseman Niklas Kronwall in front of him. Seabrook took a shot that hit Kronwall's leg and went past Howard for his first goal of the 2013 playoffs, and the first comeback from a 3–1 series deficit in franchise history.

"I don't know if I saw it go in, to be honest," Seabrook said. "I just heard the horn going and the boys jumping out. It was a pretty exhausting game, but I think I was more tired during the celebration with guys jumping and pushing me in the face and dragging me down."

The Blackhawks went on to defeat the Los Angeles Kings in the Western Conference Final, then knocked off the Boston Bruins in six games for the Cup.

6. Today's fans probably know Jeremy Roenick as part of the crew on the NHL on NBC telecasts after a playing career that saw him score more than 500 goals. But beginning with his arrival during the 1988–89 season until he was traded to the Phoenix Coyotes on Aug. 16, 1996, Roenick filled the net like few Blackhawks before him had done.

At age 21, Roenick was a 41-goal scorer for the Hawks in 1990–91; 15 of his goals came on the power play. Those numbers went up to 53 goals and 22 power-play goals in 1991–92, helping Chicago advance to the Stanley Cup Final against the Pittsburgh Penguins. He scored exactly 50 goals in 1992–93, again lighting the lamp 22 times on the power play.

Roenick "slumped" to 46 goals in 1993–94, though he put up 107 points for the second straight season. For the third straight season, he torched opponents when the Hawks had the man advantage, setting a franchise record by scoring 24 power-play goals.

But Roenick wasn't a one-trick pony. He scored at least three shorthanded goals in each of those four seasons and had a personal high of five SHGs in 1993–94.

Roenick's arrival in the NHL coincided with a career year for Dirk Graham, who had come to Chicago in a trade with the Minnesota North Stars midway through the 1987–88 season. Graham was a 20-goal scorer with the North Stars, and he finished 1987–88 with 24 goals.

That set the stage for Graham's dynamic 1988–89 season.

Graham had career-highs of 33 goals, 45 assists and 78 points under new coach Mike Keenan and set a franchise record that's nearly 30 years old by scoring 10 times while the Blackhawks were shorthanded.

Graham finished seventh in balloting for the Selke Trophy as the NHL's top defensive forward. His offensive production reverted to its former levels for the next couple of years, though he won the Selke in 1990–91 when he scored 24 goals and finished with 45 points and a plus-12 rating. He scored six times while the Hawks were shorthanded and had seven game-winning goals.

Graham spent the rest of his career with Chicago, retiring after the 1994–95 season.

7. b. You can almost draw a line through the past 60 seasons and go from one great Hawks goaltender to another with barely a break.

But even with the arrival of overtime (in 1983) and the shootout (in 2005), winning 40 games in a season is no mean feat for a goaltender. Not only do you have to be on a really good team, you have to stay healthy (Corey Crawford's appendectomy in early December blew a hole in his chance to do it in 2016–17) and get a few breaks along the way.

Glenn Hall is among the greatest goaltenders in NHL history, and he had his best years during his decade with the Hawks. That includes playing every minute of the 1961 playoffs and helping Chicago win its first Stanley Cup in 23 years.

But one thing Hall was never able to do with Chicago was finish a season with 40 wins. He led the NHL in victories three times, but never with more than 34 wins (in 1963–64 and 1965–66). Of course, Hall didn't have the luxury of getting a chance to win games that were tied at the end of 60 minutes.

The Hawks put Hall into the 1967 NHL Expansion Draft, and he was snapped up by the brand-new St. Louis Blues. However, the franchise's next goaltending star wasn't far away.

The NHL used to have an intraleague draft (sometimes called the Waiver Draft), which allowed teams to select players from other organizations with no compensation other than cash. Prior to the 1969–70 season, the Black Hawks took a flyer on a former college goaltender named Tony Esposito, the kid brother of former Hawk Phil Esposito. Tony had earned a Stanley Cup ring with the Montreal Canadiens in the spring of 1969, but with future Hall of Famers Gump Worsley and

Rogie Vachon ahead of him (and more talent in the system behind him), Esposito was the odd man out.

Talk about hitting the jackpot!

All Esposito did as a rookie was finish with a 38-17-8 record and a 2.17 goals-against average. He won the Calder Trophy, the Vezina Trophy, and was named a First-Team All-Star—pretty good for a kid who came out of nowhere.

Esposito won at least 30 games in each of the next six seasons, earning the Vezina Trophy twice and keeping the Hawks among the NHL's elite. He had 418 of his 423 NHL victories with Chicago before retiring in 1984.

Three years later, the Blackhawks took a flyer on another former college star. Ed Belfour was never drafted by an NHL team and signed with the Hawks in 1987 after leading the University of North Dakota to the NCAA championship.

Belfour got his first taste of the NHL late in the 1988–89 season, going 4–12–3 in 23 appearances. Luckily for Belfour, he remained a rookie (the dividing line was 25 games), and he came back in 1990–91 with a season for the ages.

Belfour had arguably the best rookie season of any goaltender in NHL history. He became the first Chicago goaltender to break the 40-win mark, going 43–19–7 with a 2.47 GAA. Like Esposito a generation before him, Belfour won the Calder Trophy as the NHL's top rookie. He also won the Vezina (now given to the NHL's top goaltender as voted by the general managers) and helped the Hawks win the Jennings Trophy for allowing the fewest goals.

Belfour broke the 40-win mark again in 1992–93, going 41–18–11. He had a 2.59 GAA and led the NHL with seven shutouts. He remained with the Blackhawks until being traded to the San Jose Sharks on January 25, 1997, and also played with the Dallas Stars, Toronto Maple Leafs, and Florida Panthers before retiring at the end of the 2006–07 season with 484 wins (201 with Chicago), but never came close to 40 wins again.

Crawford, a second-round pick in the 2003 NHL Draft, got three cups of coffee with the Blackhawks before sticking for good in 2010–11. He's had six 30-win seasons and led the Hawks to the Stanley Cup in 2013 and 2015—but he has yet to reach the 40-win mark.

8. Bobby Hull couldn't do it. Neither could Stan Mikita, Denis Savard, or Jeremy Roenick. Neither Patrick Kane nor Jonathan Toews has come close.

No, the only Hawk to score five goals in a game is a player most fans have forgotten.

Chicago selected forward Grant Mulvey with the 16th pick in the 1974 NHL Draft. He was able to jump right to the NHL in the 1974–75 season, finding instant chemistry with Terry Ruskowski and Rich Preston, a pair of forwards who had joined the Hawks from the World Hockey Association.

However, Mulvey wasn't much of an offensive force. In his first five NHL seasons, he never had more than 19 goals or 38 points in a season. He was abrasive and physical but not a big scorer.

That changed in 1979–80, when Mulvey put up career numbers with 39 goals and 65 points. After missing much of the 1980–81 season when he shattered his left forearm just before Christmas, he bounced back in 1981–82 with 30 goals—five of them on the greatest night a Hawk ever had.

On February 3, 1982, the St. Louis Blues came to Chicago Stadium, and the Hawks were ready for them. Mulvey opened the scoring at 10:04, and before the period was over he'd scored four times and assisted on a goal by defenseman Doug Wilson, giving him a five-point night with two periods remaining.

Mulvey assisted on a second-period goal by Al Secord, then put himself into the franchise record book at 13:46 when he scored during a power play to complete a five-goal, seven-point night that was enough to carry Chicago to a 9–5 win.

It was almost a last hurrah for Mulvey. He missed most of the 1982–83 season with injuries, played 12 games with the New Jersey Devils in 1983–84, and retired with 149 goals and 284 points in 586 NHL games—one of which Hawks fans will never forget.

9. d. The Hawks have seen the Montreal Canadiens more often in the Stanley Cup Playoffs, but they have had the most series victories against the Detroit Red Wings.

The Blackhawks and Wings have met 16 times, including four years in a row (1963–66) in the Semifinals. Chicago has won nine of the 16 series, more than against any other opponent.

Two of those series victories came in the Stanley Cup Final. Chicago defeated Detroit 3–1 in a best-of-five series in 1934 for the first championship in franchise history, and knocked off the Wings in six games in 1961 to bring the Cup back to Chicago for the first time in 23 years.

Chuck Gardiner was the hero against Detroit in 1934. He allowed two goals in the three victories and was perfect for more than 90 minutes in Game 4 before Mush March's goal at 10:05 of the second overtime gave Chicago a 1–0 victory and its first Cup.

The 1961 Final was a series dominated by the home team through the first five games, with the Hawks and Wings alternating victories (unlike the usual 2-2-1-1-1 pattern, Chicago and Detroit alternated home games throughout the series, with the Hawks having the home-ice advantage).

The series was tied 2–2, but the Hawks went in front with a 6–3 win in Game 5 at Chicago Stadium, with Murray Balfour and Stan Mikita each scoring twice. Mikita's power-play goal early in the third period broke a 3–3 tie.

It looked like the home-ice magic would continue to dominate when the Red Wings took an early 1–0 lead in Game 6 on a goal by Parker MacDonald. But Reggie Fleming scored a shorthanded goal 6:25 into the second period to get the Hawks even, and Ab McDonald's goal late in the period put Chicago ahead to stay. The Hawks blew the game open in the third period on goals by Eric Nesterenko, Jack Evans, and Ken Wharram.

The only thing that went wrong for the Hawks was the weather: A spring snowstorm canceled their flight back to Chicago.

The Original Six rivals haven't met since 2013, when the Blackhawks rallied to defeat the Wings in seven games to win their Western Conference Semifinal series. With Detroit now in the Eastern Conference, the teams won't meet again in the playoffs unless it's in the Stanley Cup Final.

10. Fans often forget that the Original Six era didn't begin until the New York/Brooklyn Americans went out of business after the 1941–42 season. From 1926–42, the NHL had as many as 10 teams, including two each in Montreal and New York.

The Americans and the Montreal Maroons are long gone, of course, but the Hawks played each of them twice in the postseason. They went 1–1 against each, but the two series victories led to a Stanley Cup.

The Hawks and Maroons faced off in a two-game, total-goal Semifinal series in 1934. The stingy defense that got the Hawks into the playoffs and carried them past the Montreal Canadiens 4–3 in a two-game, total-goal Quarterfinal series was at its best against the Maroons. The Hawks won the opener 3–0 at the Forum, putting the Maroons in a hole. Basically, all Chicago had to do in Game 2 was avoid a rout; a 3–2 victory at the Stadium was icing on the cake and sent the Hawks into the Final, where they defeated the Detroit Red Wings for the Cup.

Montreal got a measure of revenge a year later by winning 1–0 in a two-game, total-goal Quarterfinal. The teams played to a scoreless tie in Game 1 at the Forum and were scoreless through 60 minutes in Game 2. Baldy Northcott became the first player in the series to score a goal and sent the defending champs home when he scored 4:02 into overtime. The Maroons went on to win the Cup.

In 1936, the Americans knocked off the Hawks 7–5 in a two-game, total-goal Quarterfinal. New York won 3–0 at Madison Square Garden, and a 5–4 win at Chicago Stadium in Game 2 was not enough to make up the deficit.

But two years later, the teams met again, this time in a best-of-three Semifinal. The Americans won the opener 3–1 at the Garden and had a chance to sweep the series when Game 2 at Chicago Stadium went into a second overtime without either team scoring a goal. Cully Dahlstrom kept the Hawks alive when he scored at 13:01 of the second OT for a 1–0 win. Back in New York, the Hawks advanced with a 3–2 victory, then defeated the Toronto Maple Leafs in the Final for the franchise's second championship.

11. c. Artem Anisimov was originally taken by the New York Rangers in the second round (No. 54) in the 2006 NHL Draft. He spent one more season in Russia before coming to North America and spending the 2007–08 season with the Hartford Wolf Pack, the Rangers' affiliate in the American Hockey League.

Anisimov tore up the AHL in 2008–09, scoring 37 goals and finishing with 81 points in 80 games (if you're not impressed, consider that it's usually harder to put up big offensive numbers in the AHL than in the NHL). The Rangers' front office was impressed, and he was on the parent club's roster at the start of the 2009–10 season.

Anisimov spent three seasons in New York. He scored 12 goals and had 28 points as a rookie, improved to 18 goals and 44 points in 2010–11, and had 16 goals and 36 points in 2011–12, when the Rangers got within two wins of reaching the Stanley Cup Final.

But after losing to the New Jersey Devils in the Eastern Conference Final, the Rangers decided they couldn't pass up a chance to get forward Rick Nash. On July 23, 2012, Anisimov was part of the package sent to Columbus in the trade that made Nash a Ranger.

Anisimov struggled in his first season with Columbus (11 goals, 18 points in 35 games), but had a career-high 22 goals (and 39 points) in 2013–14. However, he battled injuries in 2014–15 and slumped to seven goals and 27 points in 52 games in 2014–15.

But Anisimov was soon to be on the move again. With Brandon Saad in line to get a big contract, the Hawks decided they couldn't keep him. Once again, Anisimov was part of the return package in a seven-player trade that sent Anisimov from Columbus to Chicago.

Coach Joel Quenneville put Anisimov between rookie left wing Artemi Panarin and star right wing Patrick Kane, and the trio quickly became one of the NHL's best lines. He had 20 goals and 42 points in 2015–16, doing a lot of the dirty work that helped Kane win the Art Ross Trophy as the NHL's top scorer and Panarin to take home the Calder Trophy as the top rookie. In 2016–17, he had exceeded those numbers before the end of February and finished with 45 points (22 goals, 23 assists) despite missing most of the last few weeks of the season with injuries.

12. For most of Glenn Hall's career, NHL teams didn't carry a spare goaltender; if a goalie got hurt during a game, he went off for repairs—and if that didn't work, the home team usually provided a replacement. Starting goaltenders played both ends of back-to-backs (often as part of a home-and-home series against the same opponent). The protective equipment was a far cry from what goaltenders use today, and coaching for goalies was non-existent.

That's what makes Hall's streak of 502 consecutive regular-season games so remarkable.

The streak actually began with the Detroit Red Wings when Hall took the ice for the season opener in 1955–56. The Red Wings had liked Hall enough to trade away future Hall of Fame goaltender Terry Sawchuk to make room for him.

Hall played all 70 games in 1955–56 and again in 1956–57, going 68–44–28 and leading the NHL with 38 wins in '56–57. But the Red Wings, who had won the Stanley Cup in

1954 and 1955, lost the Final in 1956 and were bounced in the Semifinals in '57, so they reacquired Sawchuk from the Boston Bruins and traded Hall to the Hawks.

Hall arrived in Chicago just as the Hawks were starting to see some light at the end of the tunnel after years of struggles. He played every game in each of the next five regular seasons and was named a First-Team or Second-Team All-Star in each of the last four.

He carried the streak into the 1962–63 season, but finally had to come out of a game on November 7, 1962, when his back stiffened up. Denis DeJordy took his place that night, and was in goal on November 10, when the streak ended at Montreal (DeJordy got the win in a 3–1 victory at the Forum).

"My back started bothering me a few days before," Hall remembered years later. "I started a game [on November 4] and figured the adrenaline would carry me through as it had in the past. This time, it would not."

DeJordy started each of the next three games until Hall returned and didn't miss a start for the remainder of the season. His streak is one NHL record that—it's pretty safe to say—will never be broken.

Often overlooked in the streak is that Hall also played 49 consecutive playoff games during that time, bringing his total streak of consecutive games to 551.

13. a. For a good part of the 1960s, it seemed like the Art Ross Trophy and the Hart Trophy had taken up residence at Chicago Stadium. Two Hawks, Bobby Hull and Stan Mikita, dominated the scoring race, winning seven times in nine seasons. That includes five in a row, from 1963–64 through 1967–68. Hull and Mikita also combined to win the Hart Trophy, given to the NHL's most valuable player, four seasons in a row—from 1964–65 through 1967–68.

Hull took home both awards in 1965–66, capping a season in which he set an NHL single-season record by scoring 54 goals and led all scorers with 97 points, also an NHL record.

In 1966–67, it was Mikita's turn. He scored 35 goals, led everyone with 62 assists, and matched Hull's single-season record of 97 points, helping the Blackhawks finish first in the regular-season standings for the first time since entering the NHL in 1926. It was Mikita's third scoring title—but in contrast to the first two, when he led the NHL in points despite taking 146 and 154 penalty minutes, he was assessed just six minor penalties and also collected the Lady Byng Trophy, given in recognition of skillful, gentlemanly play.

Mikita repeated his hat trick of awards in 1967–68, the first season of the 12-team NHL. He scored 40 goals and had 47 assists for a league-leading 87 points in 72 games (for good measure, he also led the NHL with eight game-winning goals), and took just 14 minutes in penalties.

Former Hawk Phil Esposito won the Art Ross and Hart trophies in 1968–69 when he was with Boston, beginning a stretch of 47 years in which no Chicago player captured either trophy.

That streak finally ended in 2015–16, when Kane had a career year with 46 goals and an NHL-high 106 points, winning the Art Ross as the league's top scorer and the Hart as MVP. He was 18th in balloting for the Lady Byng Trophy, but got his own hat trick of hardware by winning the Ted Lindsay Award as the league's outstanding player as voted by members of the NHL Players' Association.

14. The Triple Gold Club is an elite group of 27 players (and one coach, Mike Babcock, now with the Toronto Maple Leafs) who've been on teams that have won the Stanley Cup, the IIHF World Championship, and a gold medal at the Winter Olympics.

Toews got the first leg in 2007, when he helped Canada win the World Championship by scoring four goals and finishing with seven points in six games.

Jonathan Toews is a member of the "Triple Gold Club."

He joined the club in 2010 by helping Canada win the gold at the Vancouver Olympics, finishing with one goal and eight points (and plus-9) in seven games, then leading the Blackhawks to their first Stanley Cup since 1961 a few months later. His official entry date was June 9, 2010, when the Hawks beat the Flyers in Game 6 of the Final.

For good measure, Toews won a second Olympic gold medal in 2014 and two more Stanley Cup championships, in 2013 and 2015.

Since Toews became member No. 24, the only three additions to the Triple Gold Club have been Patrice Bergeron of the Boston Bruins (2012), Sidney Crosby of the Pittsburgh Penguins (2015), and Corey Perry of the Anaheim Ducks (2016).

15. c. The 30 four-goal games in Hawks history have been scored by 22 players, beginning with Frank Ingram on January 1, 1931, against the Philadelphia Quakers. The most recent one came when Michael Nylander scored four times at Boston on December 4, 1999.

Six players in franchise history have scored four or more goals more than once.

Hall of Famer Doug Bentley was the first; he did it in a span of just over three years in road games against the New York Rangers. Bentley scored four goals in a game at Madison Square Garden on February 22, 1944, and again on February 26, 1947.

Bobby Hull is the all-time franchise leader in four-goal games with four.

The Golden Jet scored four goals in a game for the first time against the Toronto Maple Leafs at Chicago Stadium on February 21, 1960. He did it again on February 1, 1962, this time in a road game against the Detroit Red Wings.

The last two came at Chicago Stadium in just over a month during the 1965–66 season. Hull scored four times against the Boston Bruins on December 15, 1965, and against the Rangers on January 16, 1966.

Stan Mikita had a pair of four-goal games just over three years apart. Mikita scored four times in a home game against the Pittsburgh Penguins on December 6, 1967, and against the St. Louis Blues at Chicago Stadium on December 16, 1970.

Al Secord had the longest break between four-goal games. Each of his came against Toronto at Chicago Stadium, on November 11, 1981, and January 1, 1987.

Jeremy Roenick scored four times against the New York Islanders at Nassau Coliseum on December 1, 1991, then equaled that feat in a home game against the Winnipeg Jets on February 24, 1994.

The fastest two four-goal games belong to Bernie Nicholls, who's also the only Blackhawk to score four goals in multiple road games. Nicholls scored four times against the Vancouver Canucks at Pacific Coliseum on February 5, 1995, then did it again against the Los Angeles Kings at the Forum in Inglewood, California, 19 days later.

16. The Hawks have had plenty of brother acts over the years, from the Conachers (Lionel and Roy played for Chicago; Charlie Conacher coached Roy) to the Bentleys (Max and Doug were stars; they also assisted on the only NHL goal by Reg) to the Hulls (Bobby and Dennis) in the late 1960s and early 1970s and the Larmers (Steve and Jeff) in the 1980s to four of the six Sutters at various times in the 1980s and 1990s.

The Sutters also account for the only two brothers to coach the Hawks, though one of the two never played for Chicago.

Darryl Sutter, the second-oldest of the six Sutters to play in the NHL, spent his entire playing career in Chicago from 1980–87. After coaching the Saginaw Hawks and leading the Indianapolis Ice to the International Hockey League championship, Darryl got the call to return to his old team. He served as an associate coach from 1990–92 before stepping up to the head job for the 1992–93 season.

With Ed Belfour having another outstanding season, Sutter and the Blackhawks won the Norris Division in his first season with a 47-25-12 record, only to be swept by the St. Louis Blues. Two years later, he got the Hawks to the Western Conference Final after the lockout-shortened 1994–95 season. However, he stepped down after '94–95 to return to the family farm in Viking, Alberta (a decision that enabled him to be with his son Christopher, who has Down syndrome).

Darryl finished with a 110-80-26 record and guided the Hawks to the Stanley Cup Playoffs in each of his three seasons. He's returned to the NHL and coached the San Jose Sharks, Calgary Flames, and Los Angeles Kings (leading L.A. to two Stanley Cup championships).

Six years after Darryl left, the Hawks brought in older brother Brian as coach.

Ironically, Brian Sutter had spent his entire NHL playing career with one of the Blackhawks' archrivals, the St. Louis Blues, scoring 303 goals before retiring in 1988. He went right from the ice to behind the bench, coaching the Blues from 1988–92. He also spent three seasons each running the Boston Bruins and Calgary Flames before coming to Chicago for the start of the 2001–02 season.

Brian's first season in Chicago was his most successful; Chicago went 41–27–13–1, finishing third in the Central

Division. However, the Blackhawks were eliminated in the first round of the playoffs. But the Blackhawks failed to make the playoffs in 2002–03, finishing 30–33–13–6, and after they tumbled to a 20–43–11–8 record in 2003–04, Brian Sutter's contract wasn't renewed after the lockout by new GM Dale Tallon. He finished with a 91-103-37-15 record in Chicago, the last stop of his NHL coaching career.

17. c. In baseball, a perfect game is a no-run, no-hit, nobody-reach-base performance. In hockey, it's a game where no one gets on the scoresheet—no goals, no penalties.

The Hawks and the Toronto Maple Leafs played such a game on February 20, 1944. Neither team scored and there were no penalties called by referee Bill Chadwick. It's believed to be the first such game in NHL history.

Goaltenders Mike Karakas of the Hawks and Paul Bibeault of the Maple Leafs each got credit for a shutout. Not surprisingly, the game didn't take long to play—just 1:55.

18. The 18,472 fans who packed Chicago Stadium for the NHL All-Star Game on January 19, 1991, did so only after league president John Ziegler decided the game would go on despite the outbreak of the Gulf War earlier in the week.

Coalition forces from 34 countries, authorized by the United Nations and led by the United States under President George H. W. Bush, embarked on the Persian Gulf War to liberate Kuwait, which had been invaded by Iraq. The NHL did not postpone any regular-season games, but there was the question of whether the league could (and should) hold its annual midseason gala with a war going on.

No less than Wayne Gretzky originally thought the game should be scrapped, saying that "It doesn't seem right that we're having a good time while our soldiers are risking their lives." Gretzky wasn't alone, but in the end, Ziegler decided it was Game On.

As it turned out, Ziegler was right.

Before the puck was dropped, the Stadium turned into a roaring caldron of patriotic display, with flags, sparklers, and a moment of silence. But the highlight was the fan noise that virtually drowned out Stadium singer Wayne Messmer's version of "The Star Spangled Banner." The noise rocked the "Madhouse on Madison," shaking the building to its core. Some fans were reduced to tears; even today, it's hard to watch the video of Messmer's performance and not get goose bumps.

The display of patriotism certainly made an impression on Gretzky, then a member of the Los Angeles Kings.

"I was standing next to Mark Messier during the national anthems," Gretzky said. "I said to him, 'This is unbelievable.' I've heard it as loud in here before but never this emotional. The flags of both countries, the banners, the vibrations. The sparklers, the bed sheets for troops overseas. The moment of silence. The only moment of silence. You could tell that the fans, like us, were thinking of other things. There was such a mood in that rink, such patriotism. It was good for hockey. It was a good show, period."

NBC showed the game in the United States, but it was also televised to service personnel in the Persian Gulf, and a tape was requested by Gen. Norman Schwarzkopf, commander of the coalition forces, so that the troops in the Mideast could see firsthand that the country was behind them.

The 11–5 victory by the Campbell Conference (a team that included three Hawks: Chris Chelios, Steve Larmer, and Jeremy Roenick) against the Wales Conference took a back seat to what took place before the puck was ever dropped.

19. May 15, 1967. A day that will live in Blackhawk infamy.

Phil Esposito had finished seventh in the NHL scoring race in 1966–67 with 61 points, including 21 goals, while centering a line with Bobby Hull and Chico Maki. Espo had been a key to Chicago's first-ever first-place finish during the regular season.

But the Hawks were upset in the Semifinals by the third-place Toronto Maple Leafs (the pairings back then were 1 vs. 3 and 2 vs. 4), and Esposito took a lot of the blame after going without a point in six games. Nitpickers felt he didn't have the drive needed to succeed in the playoffs and that he was too slow, too soft, and didn't finish well around the net (an astounding thought in retrospect).

Management had locked on to 22-year-old Boston Bruins defenseman Gilles Marotte, who had demonstrated some offensive skill to go along with an ample supply of toughness —he had 112 penalty minutes in 1966–67, his second NHL season.

That was the core of the trade, and it would have been bad enough were those the only two players involved. Esposito, of course, went on to become one of the most feared scorers in NHL history, setting records and leading the Bruins to two Stanley Cup championships. Marotte lasted less than three seasons with Chicago before being traded to the Los Angeles Kings.

But to make matters worse, the Hawks also included two former linemates from their Junior A team. Center Fred Stanfield and right wing Ken Hodge had yet to earn full-time NHL jobs and were likely candidates to be lost in the upcoming expansion draft that was to stock the six teams that were to begin play in 1967–68. The Hawks reportedly had received word that Stanfield, who was playing with St. Louis in the CPHL, was likely to be the first player taken by the new St. Louis Blues, and Hodge was also likely to be lost to one of the six new teams.

The Hawks wanted a center to replace Esposito, and Boston was willing to deal Pit Martin. The Bruins also included goaltender Jack Norris, since Chicago was sure to lose a goaltender in the expansion draft.

Ironically, there were "experts" at the time who wondered if the Bruins had given up too much for a bunch of underachievers. Instead, Esposito led the NHL in scoring five times, with Hodge on his right wing for most of that time. Stanfield became a reliable No. 2 center and penalty-killer who scored at least 20 goals in each of his six seasons in Boston.

Only Martin, who eventually became a fine No. 2 center behind Stan Mikita, provided much value to the Hawks.

20. d. For better or worse, the Hawks have served as the first NHL opponent for three teams since 1979.

Thanks to the addition of four teams from the World Hockey Association for the 1979–80 season, Chicago fans were the first in the NHL to get a look at Wayne Gretzky. He and the Edmonton Oilers came to Chicago Stadium on October 10, 1979, for their first NHL game. Gretzky needed less than 10 minutes to get his first NHL point (an assist on defenseman Kevin Lowe's goal 9:49 into the game).

The crowd at the Stadium probably thought it was going to be an easy night when the Hawks scored twice before the game was three minutes old, but the Oilers got even 2–2 before John Marks scored late in the period to put Chicago ahead to stay. Bob Murray added a power-play goal in the second period and Tony Esposito made 30 saves for a 4–2 win.

Thirteen years later, the Blackhawks were the visiting team when the Tampa Bay Lightning stepped onto the ice at Expo Hall on October 7, 1992, for their first regular-season game (Esposito, ironically, was working for the Lightning and was largely responsible for constructing the team that faced the Hawks that night). The brand-new Lightning made the Blackhawks look like the expansion team by scoring five goals in the first period, with Chicago scoring once on a goal by Cam Russell.

Things didn't get any better in the second period. Tampa Bay forward Chris Kontos, who had scored two of the five goals in the first period, had two more in the second to become the first (and still only) player to score four goals in a team's first NHL game. Brian Noonan's goal made it 7–2 after two periods, and a third-period goal by Michel Goulet did nothing more than make the final score (7–3) look a little more respectable.

The Lightning scored all seven goals against Ed Belfour, who faced 24 shots but made just 17 saves. It was one of the few bad nights that season for Belfour, who rebounded from his awful opening night and won the Vezina Trophy.

Belfour was in goal again on October 6, 1993, when the Florida Panthers made their NHL debut with an opening-night visit to Chicago Stadium. The Panthers took the lead 12:31 into the first period when Scott Mellanby scored the first goal in franchise history, beating Belfour during a power play.

Chris Chelios scored twice in the second period to give the Hawks a 2–1 lead entering the final 20 minutes, which turned into a wild, back-and-forth battle. The Panthers overcame deficits of 2–1 and 3–2, then took the lead when Brian Skrudland beat Belfour with 6:20 remaining. But Jeremy Roenick's goal with 3:53 remaining in regulation got the Blackhawks even, and neither team scored during the rest of the third period or the five-minute overtime, sending each team home with a point after a 4–4 tie.

The Blackhawks didn't see the San Jose Sharks until the expansion team's sixth NHL game, a 7–3 victory for the home side at Chicago Stadium.

21. The Hawks have had their way with the Buffalo Sabres during the 2010s.

From the start of the decade through the 2016–17 season, the Blackhawks and Sabres have played 11 games—and Chicago has won all 11. Six of the wins have come at the United Center, the other five in Buffalo (home of Hawks star Patrick Kane).

Five of the wins have come by one-goal margins in regulation. The Hawks also won in overtime at home on January 5, 2017, and in a shootout at Buffalo on December 19, 2015.

Kane played a big role in each of those wins against the team he grew up watching.

The Sabres actually led 2–1 entering the final minute of their 2015 game in Buffalo before Kane scored the tying goal with 33.5 seconds remaining. After a scoreless overtime, Kane scored the lone goal in the shootout.

"I get to do this once a year, and haven't done it for a couple years because I was injured last year," Kane said afterward.

"This is my fifth game here in my ninth season. It's special every time you come back. I pretty much grew up in this rink and have a lot of childhood memories. It's fun playing, fun being in this building, lot of friends, lot of family, some 88 jerseys out there. Overall when you get that finish and end up winning the game it becomes a great day."

Kane was the hero again during the 2016–17 season when his goal 56 seconds into overtime kept the Hawks perfect against the Sabres in this decade. They won 5–1 at KeyBank Center in Buffalo on February 19 to improve to 11–0–0, with Kane scoring a highlight-reel goal and setting up another tally.

"It's always fun to score in Buffalo," he said. His teammates would certainly agree.

22. The Blackhawks came into Game 2 of the 2015 Western Conference Final needing a win to avoid returning home down 2–0 in the best-of-seven series. The Anaheim Ducks had won the series opener 4–1, and a win would put them halfway to their first Stanley Cup Final since they won it all in 2007.

But the Hawks came out flying. Power-play goals by Andrew Shaw and Marian Hossa gave Chicago a 2–0 lead 6:19 into the game. But Andrew Cogliano got one goal back for the Ducks before the first period ended, and Corey Perry's goal late in the second tied the game 2–2.

That was the last goal anyone would see for a long time.

The score remained 2–2 after two periods . . . and three periods . . . and the first overtime. After four goals in the first two periods, the next 60+ minutes belonged to the goaltenders, with Chicago's Corey Crawford and Anaheim's Frederik Andersen matching save for save.

It looked like the Blackhawks had won the game 8:47 into the second overtime, when Shaw got position in front of the net as the puck ricocheted into the air. He then jumped and appeared to deliberately head the puck, which went past Andersen and appeared to end the game.

While the Blackhawks celebrated their apparent victory, it didn't take the referees long to conclude that Shaw deliberately head-butted the puck into the net. Though there's nothing in the NHL Rule Book that specifically forbids a player from heading the puck into the net, Rule 78.5 makes it clear that "when the puck has been directed, batted or thrown into the net by an attacking player other than with a stick" the goal has to be waved off.

And so the game went on.

The Hawks got a terrific performance from Crawford, who made a career-high 60 saves, including 38 in a row after the Ducks tied the game. Crawford also got some help from his posts (Anaheim hit three of them in overtime, two by defenseman Sami Vatanen).

As often happens in overtime, the winning goal came suddenly. Brent Seabrook took a shot from the right point into a bunch of bodies in front. The puck hit Marcus Kruger, who controlled it on the ice and buried the winner at 16:12, knocking Cy Wentworth out of the Hawks' record book. Wentworth had won the previous longest game in franchise history when he scored at 13:50 of the third overtime against the Montreal Canadiens on April 9, 1931.

"It's a great feeling to win," Kruger said. "We almost played two games out there and to put it in and get a big win here leaving California 1–1, we're pretty satisfied. It's going to be a great feeling stepping out there at the United Center."

23. b. In addition to being one of the most underappreciated players of his era, Steve Larmer was the Hawks' Energizer Bunny—he just kept going and going.

Larmer was practically a throwaway pick, a sixth-rounder who was taken with the 120th selection in the 1980 NHL Draft despite going 45-69-114 for Niagara Falls of what is now the Ontario Hockey League. He tore up juniors for another season, had 38 goals and 82 points in 74 games for the New Brunswick Hawks of the American Hockey League, and by the start of the 1982–83 season, he was ready to join the Hawks.

Larmer made an instant impression, winning the Calder Trophy as the NHL's top rookie by scoring 43 goals and finishing with 90 points (and a plus-44 rating). He also played all 80 games, something that would become a characteristic of his NHL career.

For the next decade, Larmer was as reliable as the sunrise: He showed up for work every day and put up consistently good-to-excellent offensive numbers while playing superb two-way hockey. He had 70 to 101 points every season and teamed with Denis Savard to form one of the best combinations in Blackhawks history.

After 11 full seasons in Chicago, he had played in 884 consecutive regular-season games, third-longest in NHL history behind Doug Jarvis (964) and Garry Unger (914), each of whom played with multiple teams during their streaks. Larmer's is the longest by any player with one NHL team.

Larmer turned 32 in the summer of 1993, and there appeared to be no reason he wouldn't pass Unger and then Jarvis for the NHL's ironman streak. As it turned out, health wasn't an issue.

Though the Hawks were one season removed from playing in the Stanley Cup Final, Larmer wasn't happy with the changes management was making—changing coaches (Mike Keenan to Darryl Sutter) and juggling the roster. He wanted to play on a Cup winner and was convinced that wasn't going to happen in Chicago.

"The team was going in a different direction and I was one of the last guys there from a different era," he told writer Tim Wharnsby. "It wasn't a rebuild. But I felt the team was stuck in neutral."

Larmer asked to be traded, and the Hawks accommodated him—but not until he had missed Chicago's first 13 games of the 1993–94 season. He wound up being reunited with Keenan when he landed with the New York Rangers as part of a three-team trade on November 2, 1993, and played an understated but vital role in the Rangers' Stanley Cup victory in June 1994.

He played one more season, finishing with 29 points (14 goals, 15 assists) in 47 games during the lockout-shortened 1994–95 season before retiring shortly before his 34th birthday.

24. c. Before he became the second-winningest coach in NHL history, Joel Quenneville was a defenseman with five teams, none of them nearly as good as the one he wound up coaching.

Quenneville was the second-round pick of the Toronto Maple Leafs, who made him the 21st player selected in the 1978 NHL Draft, no doubt having visions of a prolific scorer from the blue line after Quenneville lit up the Ontario Hockey League for 27 goals and 103 points in 66 games with the Windsor Spitfires.

After 16 games with New Brunswick of the American Hockey League in 1978–79, Quenneville got the call to the NHL with Toronto, going 2-9-11 in 61 games for a team that advanced to the Semifinals of the Stanley Cup Playoffs. He dressed for six playoff games, managing one assist.

Quenneville had one goal and five points in 32 games in 1979–80 when the Maple Leafs sent him to the Colorado Rockies (now the New Jersey Devils) along with Lanny McDonald. He played with the Rockies in their final three seasons in Denver, reaching career highs in 1980–81 with 10 goals and 34 points.

He made the move to New Jersey and played 74 games for the first-year Devils, then was traded to the Hartford Whalers in July 1983.

Coach Joel Quenneville hoists the Stanley Cup at the Blackhawks' championship celebration in 2015.

Quenneville spent the next seven seasons with the Whalers, never scoring more than six goals or finishing with more than 25 points. Quenneville had 25 points with the Whalers in 1985–86, the only season Hartford won a round in the Stanley Cup Playoffs. But he missed much of the next season with a shoulder injury, and his playing time decreased until he was sold to the Washington Capitals just before the start of the 1990–91 season. He had one goal in nine games with the Capitals before his NHL career ended.

But his next career was about to begin. The Maple Leafs signed him in 1991, and he served as a player/assistant coach with the St. John's Maple Leafs of the AHL. He stopped playing after 1992 and spent another season as an assistant with St. John's before taking over behind the bench with Springfield of the AHL for one season. He moved to the Quebec Nordiques as an assistant in 1994, made the move to Denver when the franchise became the Colorado Avalanche in 1995, and earned his first Stanley Cup ring with the Avs in 1996. He took over as coach of the St. Louis Blues midway through the 1996–97 season. More than 800 wins and three Cups later, he's still going strong.

25. Let's start with a disclaimer: The NHL didn't keep a lot of stats in its early decades, and shots on goal didn't become an officially recognized stat until the late 1960s.

That said, the Hawks have had plenty of big guns during the past 50 seasons—forwards such as Stan Mikita, Denis Savard, Tony Amonte, and Patrick Kane, among others. There have been great defensemen with big shots like Doug Wilson and Chris Chelios.

But there's been only one Bobby Hull. The leading goal scorer in franchise history is also the only Blackhawk to be credited with more than 360 shots on goal in a season.

The NHL wasn't counting individual shots on goal when Hull set the NHL single-season record with 54 goals in 1965–66. But two years later, when the league made shots on goal by individual players an official statistic, Hull was No. 1 with 364. That was 61 more than the runner-up, Mikita. He scored 44 goals, giving him a 12.1 shooting percentage.

That was just a warmup for the 1968–69 season, when Hull blew through his previous season's totals in shots and goals, finishing with 414 shots and an NHL-record 58 goals. His shooting percentage was 14.0. Ironically, that was the same percentage as the NHL's second-busiest shooter, former linemate Phil Esposito of the Boston Bruins, who had 351 shots.

Injuries limited Hull to 61 games, 289 shots on goal, and 38 goals in 1969–70. Bobby Orr of the Bruins led the NHL with 413 shots, followed by Esposito (405) and Mikita (352). Hull was fourth.

Hull was healthy again in 1970–71 and was credited with 378 shots on goal, but finished a distant third to Esposito (550), with Orr second (392). No one else in the NHL had more than 300.

In 1971–72, Hull was down to 336, again finishing third behind Esposito (426) and Orr (353). But he made the most of his opportunities, reaching 50 goals for the fifth time thanks to a shooting percentage of 14.9, his best since that stat became official in 1967.

26. c. From the NHL's early years, having one man fill the jobs of coach and general manager was, if not common, certainly not unusual. Hall of Famers such as Lester Patrick, Art Ross, and Jack Adams held down both jobs and led their teams to championships. In the 1960s, Punch Imlach built and coached the Toronto Maple Leafs to three straight Stanley Cup titles from 1962–64 and again in 1967.

The Blackhawks have had three men serve in both positions at the same time.

Tommy Ivan succeeded Bill Tobin as general manager in 1954, after he had coached the Detroit Red Wings to three Stanley Cups and six consecutive regular-season championships. Two years later, he went behind the bench himself. But doing two jobs didn't work. The Hawks were 26–56–21 in 1½ seasons with Ivan as coach and general manager before he turned over the coaching responsibilities to Rudy Pilous to concentrate on his role as general manager. By 1961, with Ivan running the front office and Pilous behind the bench, the Hawks won their first Cup since 1938.

The Hawks kept the two jobs separate until June 5, 1990, when Mike Keenan added the GM's role to his responsibilities as coach, with Bob Pulford promoted to executive vice president. Keenan, who had replaced Bob Murdoch as coach after the 1987–88 season, handled both roles for the next two seasons. The Blackhawks won the Presidents' Trophy as the NHL's top regular-season team in 1990–91 and advanced to the Stanley Cup Final in 1992.

But the Hawks were enamored of former Hawk Darryl Sutter, an assistant under Keenan, and didn't want to lose him. Sutter was promoted to coach for the 1992–93 season, with Keenan limited to the role of general manager. He left the Hawks on November 6, 1992, and resurfaced in 1993–94 as coach of the New York Rangers.

Pulford, who had served as GM from 1977–90, returned to that role through July 1997, when Bob Murray got the job. Murray was let go in 1999, and Pulford again assumed the responsibilities of general manager for the remainder of the 1999–2000 season.

He also took over as coach, at least on paper. Lorne Molleken, who had coached the Hawks at the end of the 1998–99 season and the start of 1999–2000, was technically demoted to an assistant under Pulford, though in reality, he was still running the team during games.

That ended in the summer of 2000, when Mike Smith succeeded Pulford as GM and Alpo Suhonen was named coach.

27. a. No coach wins a championship every season, but Joel Quenneville has given the Hawks the opportunity to do so in each season he's been in Chicago since taking over for Denis Savard four games into the 2008–09 season.

After a 1–2–1 start under Savard, the Blackhawks went 45–22–11 under Quenneville and came in second in the Central Division, their best regular-season finish since 1995–96. In their first trip to the playoffs since 2002 and just their second since 1997, Quenneville got the Blackhawks as far as the Western Conference Final (their longest playoff run since 1995) before losing to the Detroit Red Wings in five games.

One year later, the Quenneville-led Blackhawks ran the table, finishing with a 52–22–8 record that earned the Hawks the Presidents' Trophy as the NHL's top regular-season team, then rolled to their first Stanley Cup title since 1961.

With the salary cap forcing management to let go of players in order to stay under the cap, the Hawks made the playoffs in each of the next two seasons but were knocked off in the first round. But a rebuilt team dominated the NHL in the lockout-shortened 2012–13 season, going 36–7–5. The Blackhawks survived a second-round scare from the Red Wings and went to defeat the Boston Bruins for the second Cup of the Quenneville era.

The Blackhawks finished third in each of the next three seasons, easily qualifying for the playoffs. They got to overtime of Game 7 in the 2014 Western Conference Final before losing to the Los Angeles Kings, won their third Cup under Quenneville in 2015, and were eliminated by the St. Louis Blues in the first round in 2016.

In 2016–17, the Hawks had virtually clinched their ninth playoff berth in nine tries under Quenneville before the season had reached the All-Star Game, and they finished first in the Central Division and the Western Conference.

28. Defenseman Brian Campbell was one of the linchpins of the Blackhawks' 2010 Stanley Cup championship. He had 38 points (seven goals, 31 assists) in 68 regular-season games, then went 1-4-5 in 19 games during the Stanley Cup Playoffs and led all players in plus-minus rating by going plus-11.

The Hawks had signed Campbell to an eight-year contract reportedly worth more than $56 million on July 1, 2008, after he finished the 2007–08 season with a career-high 62 points (eight goals, 54 assists). He spent three seasons with Chicago before being traded to the Florida Panthers in the summer of 2011 as GM Stan Bowman maneuvered to keep the Blackhawks under the salary cap. The Hawks got forward Rostislav Olesz in return.

"I didn't want to leave," said Campbell, who had made his home in the Chicago area and had met his fiancée there. "That's the ugly side of the game."

After five seasons with Florida, Campbell came back to the Blackhawks in the summer of 2016, signing a one-year contract worth about $2.25 million, a lot less than the Panthers were willing to pay him to stay.

"It was my decision, it was my family's decision, and believe me, it's worth everything for me to be happy every day and to play in such a great organization and be a part of this family," he said after signing the deal to return.

Campbell has had a tremendous career for someone who wasn't highly regarded in his draft year. He played well for the Ottawa 67s of the Ontario Hockey League in his first two seasons in junior hockey, enough so that the Buffalo Sabres used their sixth-round selection (No. 156) on him in the 1997 NHL Draft.

Buffalo let Campbell stay with Ottawa for two more seasons, during which he became much more of an offensive force. Beginning in 1999–2000, he spent most of the next three seasons with the Sabres' AHL farm team in Rochester before becoming a full-time NHL regular in 2002–03. He blossomed in 2005–06, finishing with 44 points (12 goals, 32 assists), and went 6-42-48 in 2006–07.

But Campbell was scheduled to become an unrestricted free agent after the 2007–08 season, and after he put up five goals and 43 points in 63 games, the Sabres sent him to the San Jose Sharks prior to the NHL Trade Deadline.

Campbell had 19 points (three goals, 16 assists) in 20 games for San Jose and helped the Sharks advance to the Western Conference Final before the Hawks signed him.

29. The William Jennings Trophy goes to the goaltender(s) on the team that allows the fewest goals during the regular season.

To receive the award, a goaltender must play at least 25 games. The Jennings Trophy was first awarded after the 1981–82 season, when the Vezina Trophy was changed to honor the goaltender voted as the NHL's best.

Corey Crawford has put his name on the Jennings Trophy twice, though he's never won it by himself.

In 2012–13, the duo of Crawford and Ray Emery combined to allow fewer goals than anyone else. Each finished with a 1.94 goals-against average: Crawford went 19–5–5 in 30 games, with Emery finishing 17–1–0 in 21 appearances (the criteria for winning the award were prorated because of the lockout-shortened 48-game schedule; Carter Hutton started one game and was the losing goaltender).

Corey Crawford is a two-time winner of the William Jennings Trophy.

The combined total of 102 goals allowed by Chicago was two fewer than the runner-up Ottawa Senators. Crawford and Emery became the first Chicago goaltenders to win the award since Ed Belfour in 1990–91.

Two seasons later, Emery was gone and Crawford carried the load, with some help from backup goaltenders Antti Raanta and Scott Darling. Crawford was 32–20–5 in 57 appearances (all starts) with a 2.27 goals-against average. Raanta and Darling each played 14 games and were terrific backups; each finished with a .936 save percentage. Raanta had a 1.89 GAA, and Darling was at 1.94.

Together, they allowed 189 goals, matching the total surrendered by the Montreal Canadiens. This meant that Crawford had to share the award again, this time with Montreal's Carey Price.

30. c. Jonathan Toews came to the Blackhawks one year after he was the third player selected in the 2006 NHL Draft.

He played two seasons at the University of North Dakota before signing a three-year contract with the Blackhawks on May 16, 2007, skipping the last two seasons with UND to turn pro. Toews scored his first NHL goal in his first NHL game on his first NHL shot (October 10, 2007, against the San Jose Sharks) and had one point in each of his first 10 games, the second-longest streak from the start of a player's career in NHL history.

It was obvious to the Hawks at a very early stage that Toews was something special. Toews and fellow rookie Patrick Kane were two of the three finalists for the Calder Trophy, given to the NHL's top rookie (Kane won). Though he'd missed 16 games with a knee injury, Toews led all rookies in goals and was third in points.

So You Think You're a Chicago Blackhawks Fan?

Before Toews had finished his first NHL season, he'd already been named an alternate captain. On July 18, 2008, he got the captain's "C." At 20 years and 79 days, he became the third-youngest team captain in NHL history, behind Sidney Crosby of the Pittsburgh Penguins and Vincent Lecavalier of the Tampa Bay Lightning. (This feat was later surpassed by Gabriel Landeskog of the Colorado Avalanche and Connor McDavid of the Edmonton Oilers.)

The 2016–17 season was his ninth as captain. No one else in franchise history has worn the "C" as long as Toews.

31. b. The Blackhawks took Jeremy Roenick, a Boston native, in the first round (No. 8) in the 1988 NHL Draft out of Thayer Academy in Braintree, Massachusetts. Roenick spent most of the 1988–89 season with Hull of the Quebec Major Junior Hockey League before being called up to Chicago late in the season and contributing 18 points (nine goals, nine assists) in 20 games at the end of the regular season, then scored a goal and had three assists in 10 Stanley Cup Playoff games.

Roenick demonstrated that his 20-game showing was no fluke by scoring 26 goals and finishing with 66 points in 1989–90, his first full NHL season. He finished third in balloting for the Calder Trophy as the NHL's top rookie.

His scoring numbers went up again in 1990–91, to 41 goals and 94 points. He scored 15 goals on the power play, four while the Hawks were shorthanded, and finished with 10 game-winning goals. Roenick was a key part of the team that won the Presidents' Trophy as the NHL's top regular-season team, then had eight points (three goals, five assists) in six games in the playoffs, but the Blackhawks were upset by the Minnesota North Stars in the first round.

Roenick took another leap forward in 1991–92, scoring 53 goals, still a record for a Chicago center, and finishing with 103 points. He connected 22 times on the power play and had a franchise-record 13 game-winning goals. Roenick was a big contributor during the Hawks' run to the Stanley Cup Final as well, finishing with 12 goals and 22 points in 18 games.

1992–93 was Roenick's second straight 50-goal season; he scored 50 times and assisted on 57 goals for a career-high 107 points. For the second straight season, he scored 22 power-play goals, although his game-winners dropped from 13 to three.

Roenick put up 107 points again in 1993–94, this time scoring 46 goals and finishing with a career-high 61 assists. He set a franchise record with 24 power-play goals (a terrific achievement on a team that finished with a 17.5 percent success rate with the extra man) and had a career-best five short-handed goals.

The 1994–95 season was shortened by a lockout, and Roenick finished with just 10 goals and 34 points. He was limited to 66 games in 1995–96 and ended the season with 67 points (32 goals, 35 assists).

The Blackhawks traded Roenick to the Phoenix Coyotes on August 16, 1996, for Alexei Zhamnov, Craig Mills, and a first-round selection in the 1997 NHL Draft. He played for three other teams before retiring after the 2008–09 season but never put up the same kind of numbers as he did in Chicago.

32. c. There wasn't much in Bobby Hull's pre-NHL career to suggest that he would become the most feared shooter of the 1960s.

Hull played just two seasons of major junior hockey, and while he had 28 goals and 61 points in 52 games for the St.

Catharines Teepees of the Ontario Hockey Association, that's a long way from dominance in the NHL.

Still, at age 18, Hull earned a spot on the Hawks in 1957–58. He had 47 points (13 goals, 34 assists) in 70 games, finishing second in voting for the Calder Trophy as the NHL's top rookie. He bumped those numbers up to 18 goals and 50 points in 1958–59, and the Hawks made the Stanley Cup Playoffs for the first time.

Hull's big breakout came in 1959–60, when he made life miserable for goaltenders by leading the NHL with 39 goals and 81 points. There was no Maurice Richard Trophy, the award now given to the NHL's leading goal-scorer (Richard was actually in his final season as a player), but Hull did win the Art Ross Trophy as the NHL's leader in points.

After scoring "only" 31 goals in 1960–61 (but scoring four goals and 14 points to help Chicago win its first Stanley Cup), Hull took his game to another level in 1961–62. He led the NHL in goals and points for the second time, becoming the third player in NHL history to score 50 goals in a season.

By now, "The Golden Jet" was flying up and down left wing, firing 100-mph slap shots that had goaltenders cringing. After scoring 31 goals in 1962–63, he rebounded with 43 in 1963–64, leading the NHL in goals for the third time.

Though Hull dropped to 39 goals and 71 points in 1964–65, he won the Hart Trophy for the first time. He won the Hart again in 1965–66, but this time made some history along the way. On March 12, 1966, Hull became the first NHL player to score more than 50 goals in a season. Chicago Stadium erupted when Hull scored early in the third period for his 51st goal of the season. He finished with a league-leading 54 goals and also topped all scorers with 97 points.

Hull fired home 52 goals in 1966–67, helping the Hawks finish atop the league standings for the first time. He led the league again in 1967–68 with 44 goals, then broke his own single-season record and led the NHL for the seventh time by scoring 58 goals in 1968–69. He also had an NHL career-high 107 points.

Hull remained among the NHL's top scorers for three more seasons before signing with the Winnipeg Jets of the new World Hockey Association in the summer of 1972.

33. d. Few goaltenders in NHL history gave their teams the kind of play that Glenn Hall gave the Hawks during his decade in Chicago.

The Hawks caught a break when the Detroit Red Wings didn't repeat as Stanley Cup champs in 1956. Hall had led the NHL with 38 wins, but when the Wings lost to Montreal in the Final, management decided to bring back Terry Sawchuk, who had been traded to Boston two years earlier to make room for Hall.

Sawchuk's return meant Hall had to go; luckily for the Hawks, Detroit management also wanted to get rid of Ted Lindsay, one of the early proponents of a player's union. Lindsay and Hall were sent to Chicago, then mired in a playoff drought, on July 23, 1957.

Though his numbers didn't reflect it during his early seasons with Chicago, Hall was every bit as good, if not better, than he'd been in Detroit; and as the team around him improved, those numbers improved as well. Hall spent 10 seasons with the Hawks and was named a First-Team All-Star five times and a Second-Team All-Star three times. He played 502 consecutive regular-season games, an NHL record that should be safe for the ages, and was in goal for every second of Chicago's run to the Stanley Cup in 1961.

But Hall was thirty-five in 1966–67, and he played just 32 games, 12 fewer than Denis DeJordy. Though he went 19–5–5 with a league-leading 2.38 goals-against average and two shutouts, the upcoming NHL Expansion Draft and Hall's age made him a perfect candidate to be exposed for selection by the six incoming teams.

The St. Louis Blues were more than happy to take Hall, who returned the favor by helping the Blues advance to the Stanley Cup Final in each of their first three seasons. He even won the Conn Smythe Trophy as playoff MVP in 1968, even though St. Louis was swept by Montreal in the Final.

Hall spent four seasons with the Blues before retiring in 1971. He finished his NHL career with 407 wins, 275 with the Hawks.

34. b. The Black Hawks nearly had the NHL's top scorer in their first season; Dick Irvin finished with 36 points in a 44-game season, one behind league leader Bill Cook of the New York Rangers. Babe Dye finished fifth with 30 points, and his 25 goals were tied for second in the NHL with Montreal Canadiens star Howie Morenz.

It wasn't until the 1942–43 season that a member of the Hawks led the NHL in scoring, and it came from an unlikely source.

Doug Bentley hadn't scored more than 28 points in any of first three NHL seasons. But at age twenty-six, he had a breakout season, leading the NHL with a franchise-record 33 goals and finishing with 73 points, one more than Bill Cowley of the Boston Bruins.

Doug's younger brother and linemate, Max Bentley, finished third with 70 points. Reg Bentley, the oldest of the three brothers, had one goal and two assists in 12 games during his only NHL season. Doug and Max assisted on Reg's goal, marking the first time three brothers had been credited with points on the same goal.

Despite the banner seasons for Doug and Max, the Black Hawks finished fifth and missed the Stanley Cup Playoffs.

Doug Bentley upped his goal count to a league-leading 38 in 1943–44 and finished with 77 points, second in the NHL to Herb Cain of the Boston Bruins, who had a league-record 82. Doug had to do it without any help from Max, who had joined the Canadian armed forces during World War II.

Doug joined him in the military and missed the 1944–45 season. But the brothers returned from the war in time for the 1945–46 season and were teamed with speedster Bill Mosienko on a trio that became known as the "Pony Line" for its speed and lack of size. Max led the NHL in scoring in 1945–46 with 61 points, then repeated in 1946–47 with 72.

The brother act lasted until November 2, 1947, when Max Bentley was sent to the Toronto Maple Leafs in a seven-player trade. He scored more than 50 points just once but played a key role on Stanley Cup-winning teams with Toronto in 1948, 1949, and 1951. Doug remained with the Hawks through the 1952–53 season, spending most of his time on a line that included Mosienko. He didn't take part in the playoffs after 1946.

Mosienko spent his entire career with Chicago, retiring in 1955.

All three players are members of the Hockey Hall of Fame, as is Bobby Hull, the first Hawk to lead the NHL in scoring three times (1960, 1962, 1966).

35. Patrick Kane became the fifth player in franchise history to break the 100-point mark when he led the NHL with 106 points in 2015–16, but the first one to reach triple figures since 1993–94.

Bobby Hull was the only Hawk from the Original Six era to get to 100 points. Hull finished with 107 in 1968–69, the same season in which he set an NHL record with 58 goals. It was the third of Hull's four 50-goal seasons in the NHL, but the only one in which he broke 100 points.

Patrick Kane led the NHL with 106 points in 2015-16.

Hull remained the only Hawk to have a 100-point season until the early 1980s, a high-scoring era that saw the arrival of one of the game's most prolific scorers.

Montreal native Denis Savard was passed over by the Canadiens, who had the first pick in the 1980 NHL Draft, and the Hawks were more than happy to take him with the third pick. After a 75-point rookie season in 1980–81, Savard shattered Hull's record by putting up 119 points, including a franchise-record 87 assists, in 1981–82 (the NHL's highest-scoring season since World War II).

Though he was listed at 5-foot-10, 175 pounds, Savard had the speed and quickness to make life miserable for opposing defenses. He bumped up his total to 121 points (35 goals, 86 assists) in 1982–83, and after a 94-point season in 1983–84, Savard broke the 100-point mark again in 1984–85 (105) and 1985–86 (116, including a career-high 47 goals).

Savard had 40 goals and 90 points in 1986–87 before rebounding with the best season of his NHL career, scoring 44 goals and matching his career high of 87 assists to finish with 131 points in 1987–88. That's still the franchise record; in fact, Savard has the four highest single-season totals in Hawks history.

Steve Larmer spent much of the 1980s as Savard's right wing and put up some pretty good scoring numbers; however, his best offensive season came in 1990–91, the season after Savard was traded to the Canadiens. Larmer played most of the season on a line centered by Jeremy Roenick and finished with a career-best 101 points.

Roenick, who had 94 points in 1990–91, reached triple figures in each of the next three seasons. He finished with 53 goals and 103 points in 1991–92, then put up back-to-back 107-point seasons in 1992–93 and 1993–94.

Kane's 88 points in 2009–10 were the most by a Hawk since Roenick's three big seasons in the early 1990s. He enjoyed his best offensive season in 2015–16 by finishing with 106 points (46 goals, 60 assists).

36. d. The emphasis in the NHL today is on speed rather than brawn. Want proof? Of the 30 biggest single-season penalty totals in Blackhawks history, none belongs to an active player, and only one (Adam Burish's 214 PIM in 2007–08) has occurred in the 21st century.

In contrast, all nine seasons in which a Blackhawk took 300 or more penalty minutes came from 1981–82 to 1996–97.

That includes the most penalized season in franchise history.

In 1991–92, second-year left wing Mike Peluso piled up a league-leading 408 penalty minutes, shattering the franchise record of 352 set by Dave Manson in 1988–89. That total included 34 fighting majors, amazing considering that Peluso played just 63 games. It was a big jump from the 320 PIM he took as a rookie in 1990–91.

To show the difference in style of play, Peluso was called for just four minor penalties in 17 Stanley Cup Playoff games, and he had one goal, two assists, and four shots on goal during the Hawks' run to the Stanley Cup Final.

Peluso's reward for all his time in the box was a trade to the lowly Ottawa Senators that summer. His penalty minutes dropped to 318 and he had a career year offensively with 15 goals and 25 points. Two years later, he was a member of the "Crash Line" that helped the New Jersey Devils win the Stanley Cup.

Peluso and Manson (301 PIM in 1989–90, the same season Wayne Van Dorp led the team with 303) are the only

Blackhawks to exceed 300 penalty minutes in a season more than once. Bob Probert (326 PIM in 1996–97) is the most recent.

37. b. Bernie Nicholls was one of the NHL's sharpshooters during the 1980s and 1990s, finishing his career with 475 goals and 1,209 points in 1,127 games. He scored as many as 70 goals and 150 points in a single season (with the Los Angeles Kings in 1988–89).

So when the Hawks signed him as a free agent in the summer of 1994, they were undoubtedly expecting an offensive boost. The 1994–95 season didn't start until January 20, 1995, because of a lockout, and when Nicholls and the Blackhawks went into Pacific Coliseum on February 5, 1995, for their game against the Vancouver Canucks, some fans were already up in arms because Nicholls had scored just once in Chicago's first eight games.

Not even Nicholls, who had scored four goals in a game twice previously, could have guessed he'd have a night for the ages against a team that had gone to Game 7 of the Stanley Cup Final seven months earlier.

After Brent Sutter opened the scoring eight seconds into the game, Nicholls got his first of the night just over six minutes later by scoring a power-play goal. Defenseman Gary Suter made it 3–0 midway through the period with another power-play goal before Nicholls scored again at 14:26 to make it 4–0.

Canucks defenseman Jeff Brown scored before the end of the period, but Nicholls restored Chicago's four-goal lead 1:23 into the second period with his third goal of the night. Vancouver's Trevor Linden scored a power-play goal at 3:57, but

Nicholls assisted on Paul Ysebaert's goal at 5:05, then got his fourth of the game when he scored an unassisted goal at 14:45.

Nicholls had another assist in the third period, and the Blackhawks left the ice with a 9–4 victory. The nine goals came on just 24 shots; amazingly, Nicholls needed only four shots to get his four goals.

"It was fun when you have a game like this," Nicholls said afterward. "You want to play a couple of more periods."

Incredibly, Nicholls had another four-goal game before the month was over. In Chicago's 8–4 win against the Kings at the Forum in Inglewood, California, Nicholls again scored four goals, although he needed eight shots on goal this time, scoring twice in the first period, once in the second, and once in the third.

38. Believe it or not, the Hawks have actually had six games in which two players have had hat tricks.

The first two came a little more than four years apart and against the same opponent.

Doug Bentley and Bill Thoms became the first Hawks to score three times in the same game when they did it in an 8–4 victory against the New York Rangers at Chicago Stadium on February 7, 1943. Doug Bentley scored twice in the second period and once in the third; Thoms had one goal in the first period and scored twice in 59 seconds late in the third period to help the Hawks blow the game open.

In all, the line of Doug Bentley, Thoms, and Max Bentley riddled the Rangers for 15 points. Doug Bentley assisted on each of the goals by Thoms for a six-point night, Thoms had an assist on two of Doug Bentley's goals to finish with five points, and Max Bentley had four assists.

The Rangers were again the victims when the Bentley brothers fueled Chicago's 9–7 win at Madison Square Garden on February 27, 1947. This time, Doug scored four goals and had two assists for a six-point game, and Max contributed three goals and an assist.

Though Max Bentley was outscored by his brother for one night, he ended up leading the NHL in scoring with 72 points (29 goals, 43 assists). Doug Bentley finished sixth in scoring with 55 points (21 goals, 34 assists).

Nearly 16 years went by before the Hawks had two hat tricks in a game again. This time, it was the Hawks' two big guns of the 1960s, Bobby Hull and Stan Mikita, who tore up the Boston Bruins at Boston Garden on January 31, 1963.

Hull and Mikita each had their 17th and 18th goals of the season in the first period and scored their 19th of the season 25 seconds apart in the third period to complete a 9–2 blowout of the Bruins. Hull also had two assists for a five-point game—matching linemate Bill Hay, who scored the game's first goal and assisted on four others.

Mikita and Ken Wharram, two-thirds of the "Scooter Line," helped the Hawks tear up the Detroit Red Wings on February 18, 1968. Mikita and Wharram scored one goal in each period and contributed two assists for matching five-point nights in a 7–1 win at Chicago Stadium.

It was nearly 18 years before another pair of Blackhawks had matching hat tricks. Troy Murray and Al Secord celebrated the arrival of 1986 by scoring three goals apiece in a 7–4 victory against the Pittsburgh Penguins at Chicago Stadium on January 1. Murray and Secord had one goal apiece in each period. Denis Savard didn't have a goal but assisted on four—including all three of Secord's.

Linemates Steve Sullivan and Eric Daze were the most recent Hawks to have hat tricks in the same game. Each had three goals in an 8–5 win against the Bruins at the United Center on March 9, 2003. Sullivan scored two goals in the first period and one in the second; Daze had one in the second and scored two in the third. Each also assisted on two of the other's three goals.

39. Scoring goals at Chicago Stadium got a lot harder for visiting teams when Tony Esposito was taken by the Hawks from the Montreal Canadiens in the 1969 NHL intraleague draft. The Hawks set a franchise record in Esposito's first season by shutting out opponents nine times in 1969–70 (eight wins, one scoreless tie). They also had six shutouts on the road, as Esposito set an NHL rookie record with 15 shutouts.

But that paled in comparison to what the Hawks did in front of their home fans two years later.

The addition of backup Gary Smith, a solid NHL goaltender in his own right, took some of the burden off Esposito. The result was an amazing 12 shutouts in 39 home games, by far the best showing in franchise history. The Hawks also had two shutouts on the road, giving them 14 for the season. Esposito led the NHL with nine and Smith was tied for third with five shutouts despite playing just 28 games.

Equally impressive: Chicago was not shut out during the season, giving the Hawks a 14–0 record in shutout games.

The Hawks really cleaned up against non-Original Six teams. Eleven of the 12 shutouts at the Stadium and each of the two on the road came against teams that entered the NHL in the expansions of 1967 and 1970. The St. Louis Blues were shut out in three of their four visits to Chicago (and the Hawks had one of their two road shutouts at the St. Louis Arena. The Los Angeles Kings, California Golden Seals, and Vancouver Canucks were blanked twice each in front of appreciative Stadium crowds. The Philadelphia Flyers, Toronto Maple Leafs, and Minnesota North Stars each were shut out once in Chicago; the other road shutout came against the Pittsburgh Penguins.

Not surprisingly, the Hawks steamrolled their way to first place in the Western Conference and led the NHL by allowing 166 goals, 25 fewer than anyone else.

40. The Hawks picked goaltender Michael Leighton in the sixth round (No. 165) of the 1999 NHL Draft despite Leighton's 4.84 goals-against average with the Windsor Spitfires of the Ontario Hockey League.

The Blackhawks left Leighton in Windsor for two more seasons, during which he and the team improved markedly; in his final junior season, he was 32–13–5 with a 2.73 GAA.

Leighton turned pro and turned in a terrific 2001–02 season with the Norfolk Admirals of the American Hockey League, then the Blackhawks' top farm team. He spent most of 2002–03 with Norfolk until getting the call to the NHL in March 2003.

Leighton took the ice for his NHL debut on January 8, 2003, when the Hawks hosted the Phoenix (now Arizona) Coyotes and stopped 11 shots in the first period, seven in the second, and nine in the third without allowing a goal. The only problem was that at the other end of the ice, Phoenix rookie Zac Bierk was even better, surviving a 19-shot barrage by the Blackhawks in the first period and stopping all 38 shots he faced through 60 minutes to send the game into overtime tied 0–0.

Phoenix had four shots on goal in the five-minute over-time; Leighton stopped them all. Bierk did the same with the two shots he faced. With the shootout not yet used to settle ties, each team went home with a point in what turned out to be the final scoreless tie in Blackhawks history.

Leighton finished with 31 saves to become the first goal-tender to have a shutout in his NHL debut while playing in a scoreless tie. He ended up playing eight games for Chicago, fin-ishing 2–3–2 with a 2.82 GAA and a save percentage of .913.

Since then, Leighton has bounced around the NHL and AHL. However, he was on the ice for one of the most famous nights in the history of the Blackhawks. On June 9, 2010, Leighton took the ice for the Philadelphia Flyers against the Hawks at Wachovia Center (now Wells Fargo Center) in Game 6 of the Stanley Cup Final. Chicago led 3–2 in a series that had seen the home team win each of the first five games. Leighton, who had played well earlier in the playoffs but struggled against his former team in the Final, got the Flyers into overtime tied 3–3, but a goal by Patrick Kane 4:06 into overtime gave the Hawks their first Cup in 49 years.

THIRD PERIOD

A few minutes of rest, a chance to dry out the gloves and get a few words of wisdom from the coaching staff. OK, crunch time . . . we're off to the third period.

1. Tony Esposito is a Blackhawk immortal. But "Tony O" took an unusual path to the NHL for players in the late 1960s; instead of playing junior hockey, he opted to play US college hockey before turning pro. Which NCAA team did Esposito play for? *Answer on page 139.*
   a) Michigan
   b) Michigan State
   c) Michigan Tech
   d) Northern Michigan

2. Major Frederic McLaughlin was awarded the Black Hawks franchise for the start of the 1926–27 season. Unlike today's expansion teams, the Hawks (along with the other newcomers, the New York Rangers and Detroit Cougars) didn't have a whole lot of time to put together a roster. But with the Western Hockey League going out of business, McLaughlin opted to buy the core of a WHL squad and use those players to stock his new team. Which team did he buy, and how much did he pay? *Answer on page 140.*

3. Plus-minus has officially been an NHL statistic since the start of the expansion era in 1967. But being a big scorer isn't necessary to have a great plus-minus total; in fact, two of the three Hawks who've had seasons of plus-50 or better

are nowhere near the franchise's all-time scoring leaders. Who are they? *Answer on page 141.*

4. Times weren't always good for the Hawks. For much of the late 1940s and well into the 1950s, they struggled to win games and draw fans. For four seasons in the 1950s, the Hawks moved a few of their home games away from Chicago Stadium to other arenas in the Midwest. One city in particular was a popular site; it hosted a total of 11 games. Which city was it? *Answer on page 142.*

a) St. Louis

b) Indianapolis

c) Minneapolis

d) Omaha

5. Speaking of moving games . . . the NHL lengthened its schedule to 84 games in the 1992–93 and 1993–94 seasons by adding two neutral-site games for each team. Each club was the home team for one and the visitors for the other. Starting in 1995–96, the schedule was cut back to 82 games after the lockout that shortened the 1994–95 season. The Blackhawks were the home team for two neutral-site games. Where did they play and who were the opponents? *Answer on page 143.*

6. The Blackhawks have retired six numbers in honor of seven players (two players who wore No. 3 were honored). Six of the seven players are members of the Hockey Hall of Fame. Which one isn't? *Answer on page 145.*

a) Steve Larmer

b) Keith Magnuson

c) Bill Mosienko

d) Doug Wilson

7. One of those retired numbers belongs to Bobby Hull, who flew up and down left wing with the Hawks for 15 seasons. But Hull didn't begin wearing his trademark No. 9 until the 1963–64 season. He actually wore two other numbers during his first six seasons in the NHL. What were those numbers and when did he wear them? Bonus point: Why did he switch to No. 9? *Answer on page 146.*

8. Through the 2016–17 season, who was the only Blackhawks coach to win the Jack Adams Award, presented to the NHL's top bench boss? *Answer on page 147.*
a) Joel Quenneville
b) Mike Keenan
c) Orval Tessier
d) Billy Reay

9. Match the nickname to the player. *Answer on page 149.*
a) Bill Hay   i) "Elbows"
b) Eric Nesterenko   ii) "Captain Serious"
c) Glenn Hall   iii) "Red"
d) Jonathan Toews   iv) "Mr. Goalie"

10. A trade that Chicago fans have tried to forget but can't sent centers Phil Esposito and Fred Stanfield, as well as right wing Ken Hodge, to the Boston Bruins. All three went on to help the Bruins win the Stanley Cup in 1970 and 1972, and Esposito went on to earn induction into the Hockey Hall of Fame. The Black Hawks got three players, the best of whom was center Pit Martin, who wasn't Esposito but did have three 30-goal seasons and put up 90 points in 1972–73 during his 10 full seasons with Chicago. "Pit" wasn't his real name. What was it? *Answer on page 152.*

11. Joel Quenneville has been a success everywhere he's coached, beginning with his time as an assistant coach with the Quebec Nordiques/Colorado Avalanche organization (he was part of Colorado's 1996 Stanley Cup-winning team as an assistant before getting his first job as bench boss). For which team(s) does he hold the franchise record for coaching victories? *Answer on page 152.*
a) St. Louis Blues
b) Colorado Avalanche
c) Chicago Blackhawks
d) Toronto Maple Leafs

12. Against which teams did the Hawks have the most and fewest wins in a decade? *Answer on page 153.*

13. Which Western Conference rival signed defenseman Niklas Hjalmarsson to an offer sheet in July 2010, forcing the Blackhawks to match (which they did)? *Answer on page 155.*
a) Los Angeles Kings
b) St. Louis Blues
c) Vancouver Canucks
d) San Jose Sharks

14. The Hawks' all-time ledger includes games against six franchises that are no longer part of the NHL. Who were those teams and how did the Hawks fare against them? *Answer on page 157.*

15. Which of these players did NOT lead the Blackhawks in goals, assists, and points in the same season? *Answer on page 158.*
a) Kyle Calder
b) Martin Havlat

c) Ivan Boldirev

d) Jonathan Toews

16. It's difficult but not impossible to hit double figures in goals in one game. How many times have the Hawks done it, and when was the last time? *Answer on page 160.*

17. One of the best moves Rocky Wirtz made after he assumed control of the Blackhawks following the death of his father was the hiring of John McDonough as team president. Which Chicago team was McDonough working for when he was hired by the Blackhawks? *Answer on page 161.*

a) Bears

b) Bulls

c) Cubs

d) White Sox

18. There have been eight seasons in which a Blackhawk has scored 50 or more goals. They're divided among three players. Which of the three had just one 50-goal season? *Answer on page 163.*

19. The Blackhawks have had 11 seasons in which a player finished with 100 or more points. Which Chicago player came the closest to 100 points without reaching the milestone? *Answer on page 164.*

20. The Hawks' franchise record for consecutive games without a loss in regulation (wins, ties, and overtime/shootout losses) is the same at home and on the road, though they were set more than 40 years apart. How many games were involved, and in which years were the marks set? *Answer on page 165.*

21. Two members of the Hockey Hall of Fame had exactly one shutout with the Blackhawks. One is Dominik Hasek, one of the greatest goaltenders of all time. Who is the other? *Answer on page 166.*
a) Al Rollins
b) Bert Gardiner
c) Bob Sauve
d) Emile Francis

22. It's typical in the playoffs that a team will ride one goaltender. In the Blackhawks' Stanley Cup-winning years of 2010, 2013, and 2015, how many times did they use more than one starting goaltender during the playoffs? *Answer on page 167.*
a) 1
b) 2
c) 3
d) None

23. The Hawks had to juggle their goaltenders in the 1938 Stanley Cup Final because of an injury to starter Mike Karakas. Why was Karakas unable to play at the start of the series, and what did the Hawks do to compensate? *Answer on page 169.*

24. The same visiting team played in the final regular-season game and the last playoff game at Chicago Stadium. Who was it? *Answer on page 170.*
a) St. Louis Blues
b) Montreal Canadiens
c) Detroit Red Wings
d) Toronto Maple Leafs

25. One of the most important goals in Hawks history came in Game 3 of the 1961 Stanley Cup Semifinals. Chicago scored a power-play goal 12:12 into the third overtime to defeat the Montreal Canadiens 2–1. Who scored the goal? *Answer on page 171.*

26. Speaking of the 1961 Cup champs: Which Hall of Famer led the Hawks in playoff scoring that year? *Answer on page 173.*

27. The Blackhawks were the best in the West in 2016–17, winning the Central Division and finishing first in the Western Conference. Prior to that, when was the last time they'd won a regular-season division title and conference title? How many times have they finished first in each? *Answer on page 174.*

28. In the Blackhawks' 90 NHL seasons, they've used 76 uniform numbers. Which number has been worn by the most players? *Answer on page 175.*

    a) 1

    b) 3

    c) 4

    d) 6

Bonus: Which number has been, and will be, worn by only one player? *Answer on page 177.*

29. The Blackhawks had six players score 20 or more goals in 2016–17. What is the franchise record for most 20-goal scorers in a season, and when was it set? *Answer on page 177.*

30. The 1938 Hawks were one of the most unlikely Stanley Cup winners in NHL history. What made them so unusual? *Answer on page 178.*

a) Lowest regular-season winning percentage by Cup-winning team

b) Won all their home games during the playoffs

c) Won all their road games during the playoffs

d) Played last tie in Stanley Cup Playoff competition

31. Glenn Hall and Corey Crawford share the franchise record for penalty shots faced; each saw 11. How many goals did they allow? *Answer on page 179.*

32. The Blackhawks have been awarded 71 regular-season penalty shots, including one by Marcus Kruger in 2016–17. They've been successful just 16 times. Who is the only Blackhawk to score more than once on a penalty shot? *Answer on page 180.*

a) Stan Mikita

b) Bobby Hull

c) Wayne Presley

d) Jonathan Toews

33. The Hawks set team and individual records for short-handed goals in 1988–89. Which player set the individual single-season record, and how many did the Blackhawks score to set the team mark? *Answer on page 182.*

34. Hat tricks are nothing new to Chicago fans. But what is the team record for hat tricks in a season, and when was it set? *Answer on page 183.*

35. Charlie Gardiner and Corey Crawford manned the net for the Hawks eight decades apart, but they share a singular accomplishment. What was it? *Answer on page 184.*

a) Served as captain of a Stanley Cup-winning team

b) Had a shutout in Stanley Cup-winning game

c) Had five shutouts in one playoff year

d) Won three Game 7s in one playoff year

36. The Hawks struggled to win for much of the pre-expansion era. They have a lifetime winning record against just one of the other Original Six teams. Which one? *Answer on page 185.*
a) Boston Bruins
b) Detroit Red Wings
c) New York Rangers
d) Toronto Maple Leafs

37. One Blackhawks record that's safe is the mark for the most ties in a season; the last tie in the NHL was played in 2004. When was it set, and how many times did the Hawks play to a draw in that season? *Answer on page 186.*

38. Chicago goaltenders have finished with 30 or more wins 22 times in franchise history, including Corey Crawford in 2016–17. How many goaltenders have won at least 30 games in a season for the Hawks, and who needed the fewest games to do it? *Answer on page 187.*

39. The Blackhawks have been involved in 126 shootouts since the NHL adopted the tiebreaker for the 2005–06 season. How have they done, and which player has been their most successful in the shootout? *Answer on page 188.*

40. The Hawks might be the only franchise whose single-game record for assists is held by a defenseman rather than a forward. Who is he, and how many assists did he have? *Answer on page 189.*

That's it; you've made it through 60 tough minutes. But the game's still on the line. We're headed for overtime.

THIRD PERIOD—ANSWERS

1. c. Tony Esposito was one of the first players in the NHL's modern era to reach the league after playing college hockey in the US. One reason he went that route was to delay his professional debut. When Esposito was looking toward a hockey career as a goalie (older brother Phil, a center, took the more conventional route to the NHL through junior hockey), the Original Six era was still going strong and many teams basically used one goalie, limiting the number of starting jobs.

But times were changing. While Esposito was playing three seasons with the Michigan Tech Huskies (and studying business), the NHL began to prepare to go from six to 12 teams, and teams started to carry two goalies.

Michigan Tech coach John MacInnes, a former goaltender himself, recruited Esposito, who was an All-America selection and helped the Huskies win the NCAA championship in 1965, capping his first varsity season (freshmen were not eligible to play at that time). He and Rick Best were among the best goaltending tandems in NCAA history.

"We had a tremendous hockey team at that time," Esposito told the American Sports Network in 2016. "We were generally rated No. 1 in the nation by most of the coaches and polls when Rick and I played on the team."

Esposito completed his college career in 1967 and signed his first pro contract with the Montreal Canadiens in 1967.

Luckily for the Hawks, the Canadiens were swimming in goaltenders. Gump Worsley and Rogie Vachon manned the net in Montreal even after Charlie Hodge was lost to the Oakland Seals in the 1967 expansion draft. After spending 1967–68 in the minors, Esposito got some NHL playing time in 1968–69 as a backup (and earned a Stanley Cup ring) before coming to the Hawks in the 1969 intraleague draft. The rest is history.

2. It wasn't until September 25, 1926, that Major Frederic McLaughlin, a local coffee tycoon, was awarded an NHL franchise to be based in Chicago and slated to begin play for the 1926–27 season. He got the nod ahead of James Norris and fight promoter Paddy Harmon and paid the $12,000 expansion fee.

The timing didn't leave McLaughlin much time to put together a team. Opening night was scheduled for November 17, 1926. Luckily for McLaughlin, the Western Hockey League, which had competed with the NHL for the Stanley Cup, was getting ready to cease operations after the 1925–26 season (1926 was the last time a non-NHL team played in the Final).

In an effort to secure players for the upcoming season, McLaughlin purchased the WHL's Portland Rosebuds for the equivalent of $200,000 (in today's funds) and moved the nucleus of that team (players such as "Rabbit" McVeigh, George Hay, Percy Traub, Dick Irvin, and goalie Hugh Lehman) to Chicago.

McLaughlin, who wasn't a fan of the "Rosebuds" nickname for the franchise, turned his attention to finding a new one. He found the answer in his military service: During World War I, McLaughlin had served as a commander in the 333rd

Machine Gun Battalion of the 86th Division of the US Army. Members of his division called themselves "Black Hawks" in honor of the Sauk Indian chief who sided with the British in the War of 1812.

The now-famous Indian head logo was created by McLaughlin's wife, famed dancer Irene Castle.

3. It's handy to be a big scorer if you want to have a good plus-minus rating, so it's no accident that the best season in Hawks history belongs to Bobby Hull, who holds the franchise record by going plus-54 in 1971–72, a season in which he scored 50 goals and finished with 94 points.

But the other two Hawks to finish better than plus-50 made their living by keeping the puck out of their own net.

Keith Magnuson was as rugged a defenseman as there was in the NHL for much of the 1970s. With a shock of red hair, he was among the most notable players whenever he stepped onto the ice, and more than one opposing forward got dumped on his rear end when Magnuson felt he was making life a little too hard for Tony Esposito.

Magnuson was no one's idea of an offensive force; he never scored more than three goals in a season and finished his career with 14 (and 139 points) in 589 regular-season games. But he was a solid plus player through his first seven NHL seasons, and his NHL career-best plus-52 rating in 1971–72 is the second-best of any Hawk.

Bill White was a little more of an offensive presence than Magnuson; he had as many as nine goals and 47 points in a season (both came in 1972–73) after being acquired from the Los Angeles Kings prior to the 1970 NHL Trade Deadline. But his specialty was solid positional play and getting the puck to the

Hawks' stable of talented forwards. White and Pat Stapleton formed one of the best defensive pairings in the NHL—solid in their own zone and adept at not spending much time there.

In White's first full season with the Blackhawks, he had 25 points (four goals, 21 assists) and was plus-51. He and Stapleton were a big reason the Hawks made it as far as Game 7 of the Stanley Cup Final.

After finishing "only" plus-42 and plus-30 in the next two seasons, White went 5-31-36 in 69 games in 1973–74 and finished plus-51 for a second time.

Stapleton is the leading member of the "almost plus-50 club." When White went plus-51 in 1970–71, his partner was plus-49.

4. a. Given the on-ice success and sellout crowds that have become hallmarks of the Hawks for nearly a decade, it's easy to forget when times weren't so good.

Franchise founder Frederic McLaughlin, a hands-on owner, died in December 1944, and his estate sold the franchise to a syndicate fronted by longtime Hawks executive Bill Tobin. However, the actual power was wielded by James Norris, who bought Chicago Stadium in 1936, and the Norris-Tobin group paid little attention to the Hawks. After advancing to the Stanley Cup Final in 1944, the Hawks made the playoffs just twice from 1944–45 through 1957–58.

Not surprisingly, as the playoff drought grew, so did the number of empty seats in the Stadium. With crowds dwindling in Chicago, ownership began moving some home games to other cities in hopes of drawing more fans.

The first game to be moved was played in Indianapolis on December 6, 1952. The switch in venue didn't help; the

Detroit Red Wings defeated the Hawks 2–0. Despite that, Chicago made the playoffs for the first time since 1945–46.

The Hawks moved four games in 1953–54, playing three in Indianapolis and one in Omaha, Nebraska. As was the case a year earlier, playing somewhere other than Chicago didn't help the won-lost record: The Hawks lost to Detroit, the Boston Bruins, and the New York Rangers in Indianapolis and to Detroit in Omaha. They weren't much better anywhere else, finishing last with a record of 12–51–7.

The practice of playing home games in cities other than Chicago continued in 1954–55, though the locales were different. Of the eight home games that weren't played at the Stadium, six were held in St. Louis (Norris owned the St. Louis Arena) and one each in Omaha and in St. Paul, Minnesota. The Hawks finally won a "home" game away from Chicago Stadium; they defeated the Toronto Maple Leafs 3–2 on January 2, 1955, but went 1–2–5 and again finished last.

The Hawks played six games away from Chicago Stadium in 1955–56—five in St. Louis and one in Omaha. They went 1–3–2 on the way to a third straight last-place finish.

By 1956–57, all home games were again being played at Chicago Stadium. The final tally was 11 games in St. Louis, three each in Indianapolis and Omaha, and one in St. Paul. Not long after that, the Hawks, featuring homegrown stars like Bobby Hull and Stan Mikita, returned to the playoffs on a regular basis and began filling the Stadium again.

5. After the brief players strike in 1992, the NHL decided to bring hockey to non-NHL cities by having each team play two games at neutral sites throughout North America. In all, there were 50 games played in 16 cities, four of which later received NHL franchises of their own.

Each club was designated as the home team in one of its games and the visitor in the other. Most, but not all, of the games matched non-divisional opponents.

The Blackhawks (not surprisingly) were the home team when the Los Angeles Kings came to Bradley Center in Milwaukee on December 1, 1992. The game was a success at the box office, drawing 16,292 fans, but despite outshooting the Kings 47–24, the Hawks lost 6–3. It was their only loss in a 10-game stretch during which they went 8–1–1. (The Blackhawks fared no better as the "road" team; despite playing in Indianapolis for the first time in 40 years, they lost 4–1 to the Washington Capitals in front of less than 8,800 fans.)

Chicago's two neutral-site games in 1993–94 were played exactly a month apart, and each involved a trip out west.

The Hawks went to Arco Arena in Sacramento, California, on February 8 as the visiting team for a game against the San Jose Sharks. Chicago trailed 4–1 before goals by Patrick Poulin and Eric Weinrich cut the deficit to one, but the Sharks hung on for a 4–3 win. It was one of three losses to the Sharks during a nine-game, three-week road trip.

On March 8, the Hawks went to America West Arena in Phoenix, where they were the home team against the Mighty Ducks of Anaheim. Joe Murphy scored two goals and Ed Belfour made 31 saves in a 3–0 victory. Three nights later, and with the home and road roles reversed, the Hawks won 3–2 at Anaheim.

Happily for a lot of players, the extra two games were dropped as part of the collective bargaining agreement that settled the 1994–95 lockout. The schedule has remained at 82 games since then.

6. b. The banners that hang above the ice at the United Center honor some of the greatest players in NHL history.

Stan Mikita and Bobby Hull are top-tier Hall of Famers. So are Glenn Hall and Tony Esposito, two of the greatest goaltenders in hockey history. Denis Savard was one of the most spectacular offensive players the NHL has ever seen. Pierre Pilote was one of the best defensemen of the 1960s and a three-time Norris Trophy winner.

Pilote wore No. 3 for most of his time with the Hawks until being traded after the 1967–68 season (he played one season with the Toronto Maple Leafs before retiring). One year later, No. 3 was issued to a 22-year-old defenseman named Keith Magnuson, who was trying to make the Hawks after playing three seasons at the University of Denver.

In an era where more and more defensemen were rushing the puck and joining the play, Magnuson was a stay-at-home guy whose most notable attribute was his toughness. He played all 76 games in 1969–70 and didn't have a goal (he did contribute 24 assists), but Magnuson led the NHL with 213 penalty minutes.

He did score three goals and finish with 23 points in his second NHL season. But more notable was his 291 penalty minutes, by far the most in the league (Dennis Hextall of the California Golden Seals was second with 217).

A lot of those penalty minute came as the result of fighting majors—Magnuson got some media attention when it was revealed that he had taken boxing lessons. But he was also solid in his own zone and made the NHL All-Star Game twice (1971 and 1972).

Magnuson called it a career after playing three games in the 1979–80 season; he had just 14 goals and 139 points in

589 games, but piled up 1,442 penalty minutes. He was named coach of the Black Hawks for the 1980–81 season, but was let go the following season.

In 1987, Magnuson was one of the founders of the Blackhawks Alumni Association and served as its first president. He died in an auto accident on December 15, 2003. On November 12, 2008, the Hawks retired No. 3 in honor of Magnuson and Pilote. Magnuson is still the only non-Hockey Hall of Fame member whose number has been retired by the Hawks.

7. When you think of Bobby Hull, the vision of a blond-haired Adonis speeding down left wing wearing No. 9 comes immediately to mind. Hull is as identified with No. 9 in Chicago as Gordie Howe is in Detroit and Maurice Richard in Montreal.

But when Hull arrived in the NHL in 1957, he was given No. 16, which had been worn by Johnny Wilson during the previous season. No. 9 was being worn by another forward,

Bobby Hull (center) didn't always wear No. 9 with the Hawks.

Nick Mickoski; when Mickoski was traded to the Detroit Red Wings in December, one of the players who came back in the trade, Earl Reibel, was given No. 9.

Hull had some great success wearing No. 16. In 1959–60, he led the NHL in goals for the first time and was named a First-Team All-Star. In 1960–61, he played a key role in the Hawks' first Stanley Cup championship since 1938.

As he recounted in his book, *The Golden Jet*, Hull switched to No. 7 in the 1961–62 season, and he wore that number when he scored 50 goals in a season for the first time. Hull also wore No. 7 for the 1962–63 season.

But at training camp before the 1963–64 season, Hull finally received the number that became synonymous with him.

"I was given No. 9 by Walter "Gonzo" Humeniuk, our trainer and equipment man, who told me I was better than the other No. 9s, Gordie Howe and Rocket Richard. That was a stretch, but I was honored to be mentioned in the same breath as them, to be honest. Little did I imagine then that the Blackhawks would retire the No. 9 jersey many years later."

Hull wore No. 9 for the rest of his time in Chicago.

Ironically, when he returned to the NHL for the 1979–80 season with the Winnipeg Jets and was traded to the Hartford Whalers during the season, Hull had to wear No. 16 again. The reason: Howe was already wearing No. 9.

8. c. The Jack Adams Award, named in honor of the Detroit Red Wings' longtime bench boss, is the NHL's coach of the year award—officially, it's given to the coach "adjudged to have contributed the most to his team's success." The winner is selected by a poll of the National Hockey League Broadcasters

Association at the end of the regular season. The award has been given out since 1974, when it was won by Fred Shero of the Philadelphia Flyers.

Five men have won the Jack Adams more than once; Pat Burns is the only one to win it three times (with three different teams).

Unfortunately for Billy Reay, one of the great coaches in NHL history, his prime seasons with the Hawks came before the award was instituted. It's hard to believe he wouldn't have won at least once (almost certainly in 1966–67, when the Hawks won the Prince of Wales Trophy as the regular-season champion for the first time in their history). By the time the Adams was first given out in 1974, Chicago's run of four straight first-place finishes was ending, and by the time he left early in the 1976–77 season, the Hawks were a middle-of-the-pack team.

Mike Keenan won the Jack Adams in 1984–85, when he led the Philadelphia Flyers to first-place finish and all the way to the Stanley Cup Final. The Flyers let him go after 1987–88, and the Hawks wasted no time bringing him to Chicago. The Hawks finished fourth in the Norris Division during the regular season but won two playoff rounds before losing to the Calgary Flames in the Campbell Conference Final.

Keenan led the Blackhawks to first place in the Norris Division in each of the next two seasons; they advanced to the conference final again in 1990 but were upset by the Minnesota North Stars in the first round in 1991.

The Blackhawks dropped from 106 points to 87 in 1991–92, finishing second in the Norris, but went on a roll in the playoffs and won 11 consecutive games to advance to the Stanley Cup Final, However, the defending champion Pittsburgh

Penguins were on a roll of their own and swept the series. Keenan didn't return as coach.

Quenneville has been behind the bench for what's arguably been the most successful stretch in franchise history. He's led the Blackhawks to three first-place finishes in the Central Division and three Stanley Cup championships—but has never won the Jack Adams Award with the Blackhawks. He did win it in 1999–2000 with the St. Louis Blues.

He's almost forgotten now, but Orval Tessier is the only coach in franchise history to be honored with the Adams award. Tessier paid his dues as a junior coach, then led the New Brunswick Hawks to the AHL's Calder Cup in 1982.

That led to a promotion, and Tessier's first season in the NHL was a smash. Tessier took over a team that had finished with 72 points in 1981–82 and led Chicago to first place in the Norris Division. The Hawks defeated the St. Louis Blues and the North Stars in the first two rounds of the playoffs, but they were no match for the Edmonton Oilers, who swept them in four games.

Chicago's 47–23–10 record was enough to earn Tessier the Jack Adams Award.

Unfortunately, Tessier was the coaching equivalent of a one-hit wonder. Chicago dropped to 68 points (30–42–8) in 1983–84 and lost in the first round of the playoffs. The Hawks were 22–28–3 after 53 games in 1984–85 when Tessier was fired. He never coached in the NHL again, though he did earn a Stanley Cup ring in 2001 as a scout with the Colorado Avalanche.

9. His real name was Bill Hay, but a lot of fans and writers called the 1960 Calder Trophy winner "Red." He was, after all, a redhead. Even hockey cards had his name as Bill "Red" Hay, though in the book *Tales From the Chicago Blackhawks Locker Room*, by Harvey Wittenberg, he's listed as Bill "Don't call me Red" Hay.

Either way, Hay was a key contributor to the Hawks during the final years of the Original Six era. He spent much of that time as center of the "Million Dollar Line" with Bobby Hull and Murray Balfour.

Hay starred in two seasons at Colorado College, leading the Tigers to the NCAA title in 1957. Though it was almost unheard of at the time for a college player to make it in the NHL, Hay opted to try and found a home with the Hawks, who had acquired his rights from the Montreal Canadiens.

Hay was one of the best stickhandlers and playmakers in the NHL. He often quarterbacked the power play and became a leader; in only his second season with the team he was named an alternate captain.

He was a consistent point producer before deciding to retire following the 1965–66 season. General manager Tommy Ivan talked him into returning during the 1966–67 season, and he helped the Hawks finish first for the first time in franchise history. The Hawks didn't protect him in the 1967 Expansion Draft, and he was selected by the St. Louis Blues but opted to retire and go into the family oil business. He spent more than three decades in various positions at the Hockey Hall of Fame, and was inducted as a builder in 2015.

Eric Nesterenko earned the nickname "Elbows" for his skill in the corners. He was a player who would be known today as an agitator, but he also contributed offensively, reaching double figures in goals 12 times in 16 seasons with Chicago after being acquired for cash on May 21, 1956. That includes the 19 goals he scored in 1960–61 while playing on a line with Tod Sloan and Ron Murphy. The threesome's solid two-way play helped the Hawks win the Stanley Cup for the first time in 23 years.

Nesterenko finished his NHL career with 574 points (250 goals, 324 assists) in 1,219 games. In 1986, he played the father of Dean Youngblood (played by Rob Lowe) in the movie *Youngblood*, and also served as the film's hockey consultant.

Few nicknames were more perfect than Glenn Hall's. His 2002 biography, *The Man They Call Mr. Goalie*, said it all. He earned the nickname partly because of his acrobatic style but largely due to his grit.

Hall was one of the greatest goaltenders in NHL history. He won the Calder Trophy in 1956 with the Detroit Red Wings but is best-known for his 10 seasons with the Hawks, where he helped Chicago end a 23-year Stanley Cup drought by winning in 1961. Three times he won or shared the Vezina Trophy, then given to the goaltender(s) on the team that allowed the fewest goals.

Hall was inducted into the Hockey Hall of Fame in 1975, but his influence on the game lives on. He was one of the first practitioners of the butterfly style of goaltending, which dominates the game today.

Jonathan Toews, who received the "C" at age twenty, picked up the nickname "Captain Serious" for his no-nonsense approach to hockey. Though credit for the name varies (in 2009, *Sports Illustrated* reported that Toews himself attributes it to teammate Brent Seabrook), it was a perfect fit—he was an old soul in a young body.

Toews was an elder statement practically before he could legally go out for a postgame beer with his teammates. But though the "Captain Serious" nickname has traveled with him, it's become less accurate as he's matured and mellowed.

He's even learned to laugh at himself a bit. In a public service announcement video released by the Hawks in 2015, he plays off his nickname and reputation to admonish fans who opt to leave their seats for the restroom when play is going on.

10. May 15, 1967, is the day Chicago sent future Hall of Famer Phil Esposito and two other solid players to the Boston Bruins. The key piece that came back in return was supposed to be defenseman Gilles Marotte, but the most valuable one turned out to be center Hubert "Pit" Martin (the nickname came from a popular French comic strip character).

Martin wasn't anywhere close to Esposito—not in size (5-foot-8, 165 pounds), style of play (speed, rather than strength), nor production (reliable, not spectacular). But while Marotte was traded (to the Los Angeles Kings) less than three years after arriving in Chicago, Martin was a solid center for a decade, most of which was spent centering the "MPH Line" with left wing Dennis Hull and right wing Jim Pappin. He scored 30 or more goals three times, put up 90 points in 1972–73, and had three other seasons with 70 or more points.

Martin played in the NHL All-Star Game in four consecutive years (1971–74), won the Bill Masterton Trophy in 1970, and helped the Hawks advance to the Stanley Cup Final in 1971 and 1973.

Tragically, he died on November 30, 2008, when his snowmobile plunged into an icy lake in northwestern Quebec. The Hawks had been planning to honor Martin and his linemates later in that season.

11. a. Joel Quenneville could well end his coaching career owning most of the Hawks' records. He's already the only coach in franchise history to win multiple Stanley Cups and trails only Scotty Bowman on the NHL's all-time wins list.

But regardless of whether he eventually owns the Hawks' record for all-time wins, he's already the franchise leader for one of Chicago's biggest rivals.

After apprenticing as an assistant with the Colorado Avalanche, Quenneville got his first job as coach with the St. Louis Blues midway through the 1996–97 season. He helped them qualify for the Stanley Cup Playoffs with a record of 18–15–7, enough for a fourth-place finish in the Central Division, though they lost their first-round playoff series.

The Blues continued to climb under Quenneville, earning the Presidents' Trophy in 1999–2000 with a 51–19–11–1 and an NHL-best 114 points. Quenneville won the Jack Adams Award as coach of the year; however, St. Louis lost to the San Jose Sharks in the first round.

Quenneville then led the Blues to three consecutive second-place finishes in the Central Division. They got as far as the Western Conference Final in 2001 before losing to the Avalanche, who went on to win the Cup. The Blues lost in the second round in 2002 and the first round in 2003. They were 29–23–7–2 after 61 games in 2004 when Quenneville was fired, but his 307 victories are still the most in Blues history.

After three seasons coaching the Avalanche, Quenneville was fired again. He joined the Hawks as a pro scout in September 2008, replaced Denis Savard as coach in October, and has led the Hawks to the playoffs in each of his nine seasons in Chicago.

12. Not surprisingly, the Hawks' best and worst records against an opposing team came from the Original Six era, when a team played each of its five rivals 14 times apiece.

Chicago had a field day in the 1960s against the NHL's two weakest teams. Chicago went 70–36–18 against the Boston Bruins and 69–35–20 against the New York Rangers, earning 158 points against each. Neither the Bruins nor the Rangers had much success for most of the 1960s, though each was on the upswing as the decade ended.

The Hawks cleaned up on the NHL's two weaklings most blatantly in 1962–63, going 10–2–2 against the Bruins and Rangers. They were actually 10–0–2 through their first 12 games against New York before losing the last two.

Chicago's best single-season showing against any team came against the Bruins in 1966–67. One of the big reasons the Hawks finished in first place for the only time in the pre-expansion era was that they beat up on the Bruins, finishing 11–2–1 in 14 games. Not only did the Hawks win, but they often won big, outscoring Boston 59–28—including a 10–2 win at Boston Garden on December 11, 1966.

The Hawks' success in the 1960s came after they had consistently served as a punching bag for the NHL's elite teams in the 1950s. No team beat up on Chicago more than the Montreal Canadiens, who won the Stanley Cup six times in the decade—including five in a row.

The Canadiens and Hawks played 140 times during the 1950s; Chicago won just 22 of those games, lost 90, and tied 28.

The Hawks went 1–10–3 against Montreal in 1952–52; then things got really bad. Chicago was 0–11–3 in 14 games against the Canadiens in 1954–55 (they were 0–5–0 at the Stadium, 0–6–1 in Montreal, and tied two "home" games that were played in St. Louis and Omaha, Nebraska, respectively).

The 1955–56 season wasn't much better: Chicago went 1–12–1 and lost the final 11 games, being outscored 49–13. Chicago also went 1–8–5 against Montreal in 1958–59.

Not surprisingly, Hawks fans really savored the victory against Montreal in the 1961 Semifinals—it was at least a small measure of payback!

13. d. One hallmark of smart management in the salary-cap era is knowing which players you want to keep and which you (reluctantly, in many cases) must be willing to allow to go elsewhere. Such was the case with defenseman Niklas Hjalmarsson.

Hjalmarsson was Chicago's fourth-round pick (No. 108) in the 2005 NHL Draft. He came to North America in 2007 and had two stints with the Hawks before making it for good in 2009–10. He had 17 points (two goals, 15 assists) in 77 games, then contributed eight points (one goal, seven assists) in 22 games to help the Blackhawks win the Stanley Cup.

Hjalmarsson picked the right time to become a restricted free agent. Very few RFAs get offers from other teams, but on July 9, 2010, Hjalmarsson signed an offer sheet with the San Jose Sharks, the team Chicago had swept in the Western Conference Final. Hjalmarsson became the first defenseman in 13 years to receive an offer sheet. Chicago had a week to match, but it took just three days for the Hawks to announce that they would do just that.

The decision to keep Hjalmarsson meant that the Hawks wouldn't have enough room under the salary cap to re-sign goaltender Antti Niemi, who had just backstopped them to their first Cup since 1961. Niemi, who went 16–6 with a 2.63 goals-against average, a .910 save percentage, and two shutouts, signed with the Sharks less than two months later.

Niklas Hjalmarsson was part of three Stanley Cup-winning teams with the Blackhawks.

Hjalmarsson continued to excel for the Hawks as a second-pair defenseman who could move the puck but usually did his best work in his own zone. He never had more than 26 points in any season with Chicago, and his five goals in 2016-17 were a career high. But Hjalmarsson was a plus player in every one of his eight full seasons with the Hawks until he was traded to the Arizona Coyotes on June 23, 2017.

14. No defunct team had more games against the Blackhawks than the New York/Brooklyn Americans, who became the Big Apple's first NHL team when they entered the NHL in 1925 but were soon overshadowed by the New York Rangers, who arrived one year later. The teams played their home games at Madison Square Garden, but the Americans were tenants while the Rangers were owned by MSG.

The Hawks barely finished with a winning record against the Americans, who were based in Brooklyn for their final season in the NHL (1941–42) before folding. The Hawks were 26–13–8 against the Americans at Chicago Stadium but just 15–23–9 in New York for a combined record of 41–36–17. The teams also split two playoff series.

The Montreal Maroons gave the Hawks a lot of trouble before folding after the 1937–38 season. Chicago went 23–30–9 against the Maroons, largely because of their 8–20–3 showing at the Forum (a place where the Hawks also struggled to win when playing the Canadiens). As was the case with the Americans, the Hawks and Maroons split two playoff series.

The Maroons were one of two NHL franchises that won the Stanley Cup before going out of business. The other was the Ottawa Senators, one of hockey's early dynasties and the team that won the Stanley Cup in 1926–27, the Hawks' first season in the NHL. Chicago finished 15–11–6 against the Senators before the franchise relocated to St. Louis for the 1934–35 season. Chicago was 4–1–1 against the St. Louis Eagles in their only season in the NHL before the franchise folded.

The Hawks were perfect against another one-year franchise, the Philadelphia Quakers, going 6–0–0 in 1930–31. They didn't fare as well against another Pennsylvania-based franchise, the Pittsburgh Pirates, finishing 11–12–1 in four seasons. The Pirates were the only defunct team with a winning record in Chicago (6–5–1).

The most recent Hawks opponent that no longer exists is the California Seals/Cleveland Barons. The Seals, based in Oakland, were part of the "Second Six" expansion in 1967 but struggled to draw fans, moved to Cleveland in 1976, and merged with the Minnesota North Stars two years later.

Chicago Stadium was one of the Seals' least-favorite places to visit; the Hawks were 17–4–2 in 23 home games and also went 10–9–5 on the road. The Barons did somewhat better, splitting eight games with Chicago during their two NHL seasons (3–1–0 in Cleveland, 1–3–0 in Chicago).

15. d. You don't have to be a star to lead a team in the major scoring categories—goals, assists, and points. It doesn't hurt, but it's not a must. Conversely, some stars may not have the kind of balanced scoring line that would lead all three categories.

Kyle Calder had a career year in 2005–06, finishing with 59 points (26 goals, 33 assists) to lead the Hawks in all three categories on a team that finished fourth in the Central Division. His reward was to be traded to the Philadelphia Flyers during the summer of 2006 for center Michal Handzus after winning his arbitration case.

Calder had never put up more than 21 goals or 53 points before 2005–06, and he never came close to those numbers again. By 2009–10, he was no longer in the NHL; he played in the AHL, ECHL, and KHL until retiring in 2012.

After missing most of the 2005–06 season with a shoulder injury, Martin Havlat was traded to the Hawks by the Ottawa Senators on July 10, 2006. Havlat had a solid first season in

Chicago, leading the team in all three categories with 25 goals, 32 assists, and 57 points (Patrick Sharp was next in goals with 20, Havlat was the only player with 30 or more assists, and Radim Vrbata was second with 41 points).

Havlat was hurt for much of 2007–08, but he stayed healthy in 2008–09 and had a career year with 77 points (29 goals, 48 assists), helping the Hawks return to the playoffs and get as far as the Western Conference Final. His timing was perfect; Havlat was eligible for unrestricted free agency that summer and signed with the Minnesota Wild. However, Havlat was plagued by injuries through the rest of his career.

Ivan Boldirev was an underrated scorer throughout his NHL career, which included nearly five full seasons in Chicago (1974–79). In 1976–77, his third season with the Hawks, he and Darcy Rota tied for the team lead with 24 goals and led the Hawks with 38 assists and 62 points.

In 1977–78, he led across the board with 35 goals, 45 assists, and 80 points, helping the Hawks finish first in the Smythe Division. Boldirev was leading the Hawks in scoring again in 1978–79 when he was dealt to the Atlanta Flames as part of a nine-player trade late in the season. His 29 goals and 64 points in 66 games were still the best on the team. Boldirev played through the 1984–85 season, retiring with 866 points (361 goals, 505 assists) in 1,052 games.

Jonathan Toews has more name recognition than Calder, Havlat, and Boldirev put together. But they've done one thing he hasn't—lead the Hawks across the board in scoring. In fact, Toews has never led the Hawks in goals or assists; however, he did lead them in points twice (76 in 2010–11 and 66 in 2014–15). Rest assured that a handful of Stanley Cup rings more than makes up for any personal honors.

16. Beginning with a 10–3 demolition of the Philadelphia Quakers on January 1, 1931, the Hawks have scored 10 or more goals 18 times since joining the NHL in 1926. All but three of those games were played at home, and Chicago scored exactly 10 goals in 16 of the 18.

(One game probably deserves an asterisk: The Hawks defeated the Montreal Canadiens 10–2 at Chicago Stadium on April 5, 1970, but five of the goals were scored into an empty net after Montreal pulled its goaltender to try to score enough goals to catch the New York Rangers for the final playoff berth in the East.)

After the rout of the Quakers, it was more than nine years before the Hawks hit double figures again; it happened in a 10–1 victory against the Canadiens on February 22, 1940. They hit double figures twice against the New York Rangers in 1943—10–1 on January 28 and 10–5 on November 14.

The next four came against the Boston Bruins. Chicago won 10–4 on October 30, 1949, and 10–2 on February 17, 1955, then hit double figures twice in just over a year at Boston Garden: 10–1 on December 4, 1965, and 10–2 on December 8, 1966.

The Hawks set the franchise record for goals in a game not in Chicago but in Philadelphia, winning 12–0 at the Spectrum on January 30, 1969.

Not surprisingly, the offense-happy 1980s contributed the most double-figure games—five. That includes an 11–3 victory against the Hartford Whalers on November 23, 1980, the most goals the Hawks have scored in a home game. The last two came against the Winnipeg Jets, who lost 10–3 on December

15, 1982, and 10–1 on October 12, 1988, which was the last time Chicago has scored 10 or more goals in a game.

17. c. The hiring of John McDonough as president of the Hawks was one of the events that marked a turning point for the franchise.

McDonough, a Chicago native, came to the Hawks from the Chicago Cubs as president on November 20, 2007 (he added the title of CEO in 2011), and has been a cornerstone to the revival of the franchise on and off the ice.

It's easy for fans who are accustomed to watching stars like Patrick Kane and Jonathan Toews skate in front of packed houses at the United Center to forget what the Hawks were like when owner Rocky Wirtz hired McDonough shortly after taking the reins following the death of his father. The on-ice product wasn't very good—the Hawks had made the Stanley Cup Playoffs just once since 1997 and hadn't won a series since 1996. Not surprisingly, fans stayed away; the United Center was half-full on many nights. Home games weren't on TV (William Wirtz, Rocky's father, believed showing home games would cut down ticket sales), and the Hawks had dropped to the bottom of the Chicago sports scene.

"I really didn't know what to expect when I started," McDonough told *The Athletic* in December 2016. "I think the franchise was in a more dire situation than I thought, and we had to make a lot of changes. We had to make some unpopular decisions on popular people, obviously. But we had to build an organization from the ground up. I wanted to hire young, dynamic, enthusiastic people that have never been a part of anything like this before. And it wasn't necessarily hell bent on pitching up a tent in the Ivy League.

"I wanted to hire a bunch of humble, hungry walk-ons that really understood the importance of relationships and achievements and exceeding expectations. I kind of like a work environment comfortably uncomfortable. I like to challenge people. I'm very much in favor of innovation and creativity and never, ever, ever, ever being satisfied or tethered to something that we've always done it this way."

The Hawks went 40–34–8 in McDonough's first season as president, and two years after that, they were hoisting the Stanley Cup. Home games were put on television, the fans returned, and the Hawks have become one of the hottest tickets in Chicago—their sellout streak passed 400 games in 2016–17 and the season-ticket base climbed from 3,400 to more than 14,000. The 2016–17 season marked the ninth consecutive season in which the Hawks led the NHL in attendance.

McDonough has also been instrumental in bringing marquee events to Chicago. That includes the 2009 NHL Winter Classic between the Blackhawks and Detroit Red Wings at Wrigley Field, the 2014 Stadium Series game between the Blackhawks and Pittsburgh Penguins at Soldier Field, the NCAA Frozen Four in April 2017, and the NHL Draft in June 2017. In addition, he instituted the annual Blackhawks Convention, the first event of its kind in the NHL and a huge hit with fans.

Despite all that success, McDonough made it clear to *The Athletic* that he and the Hawks are taking nothing for granted.

"I think sometimes people get the impression that every day here is Camelot, and it's anything but," he said. "It can get thorny here from time to time. We challenge each other. It's very, very healthy. It's very respectful. But there's a dynamic here that none of us are caught up in winning three Stanley

Cups. That's not something we reference, talk about. We do talk about everything we can do to win the next one and creating a great environment for our fans.

"You know we had a lot of ground to make up. We were off the radar for a couple decades."

18. Bobby Hull made scoring 50 goals look easy—he did it five times from 1961–62 through 1971–72. Jeremy Roenick did it in back-to-back seasons (1991–92 and 1992–93).

Hull and Roenick each finished with more than 500 goals, so it's not surprising that each had multiple 50-goal seasons. But the other Hawk to get 50 in a season has largely faded into history.

Al Secord was a forward in his third season with the Boston Bruins when the Hawks acquired him in a trade for defenseman Mike O'Connell on December 18, 1980. He had 22 points (13 goals, nine assists) in 41 games with the Hawks. Perhaps more notable was his 145 penalty minutes; it was the fourth straight season in which he'd had at least 125 PIM. The Bruins often appeared more interested in Secord's penalty numbers than his scoring figures.

But beginning in the 1981–82 season, the Hawks put Secord on a line centered by Denis Savard. Playing with one of the NHL's best passers jump-started Secord's career: He scored 44 goals and finished with 75 points. Secord piled up 303 penalty minutes, becoming the first player in NHL history to score 40 or more goals while taking 300 or more penalty minutes.

"I was playing with Denis Savard regularly," he told greatesthockeylegends.com. "My presence gave him more time to operate on ice and I got more ice time than ever before. I played a really physical game that year and I fought quite a bit.

Even though I had a lot of penalty minutes that year, I never thought I got penalties because of my reputation. The referees respected me and I respected them."

Secord was even better in 1982–83. With the arrival of rookie Steve Larmer completing what became known as the "Party Line," Secord tied Hull for the second-highest single-season goal total in franchise history by scoring 54 times (and reduced his PIM total to 180. He led the NHL with 20 power-play goals.

Unfortunately for Secord and the Hawks, his career was derailed by injury. He missed most of the 1983–84 season with torn abdominal muscles and was limited to 51 games during the following season with pulled muscles in his thigh.

Secord was healthy again in 1985–86 and scored 40 goals for the third time in his career. But he continued to be hampered by injuries. The Hawks traded him to Toronto on September 3, 1987; he also played for the Philadelphia Flyers before returning to Chicago for the 1989–80 season, his last in the NHL.

19. It's like batting .299 instead of .300 in baseball or averaging 19.9 points instead of 20 in basketball: Finishing an NHL season with 99 points is a tremendous accomplishment that would have gotten a lot more attention had it been one point more.

Such was the fate of Hawks center Troy Murray in 1985–86.

Murray had become one of the NHL's best No. 2 centers behind Denis Savard and was still just twenty-three years old when the 1985–86 season began. Playing on a line with Curt Fraser and Eddie Olczyk, Murray enjoyed a breakout year, finishing with 99 points (45 goals, 54 assists). More impressive was the fact that in addition to his scoring numbers, Murray won the Selke Trophy as the NHL's top defensive forward.

Though he never approached those offensive numbers in a career that lasted another decade, Murray was one of the best two-way centers of his era. He retired in 1996 after helping the Colorado Avalanche win the Stanley Cup in their first season in Denver. In all, he played 915 NHL games and had 584 points (230 goals, 354 assists)—including the 100-point season that almost was.

20. The Blackhawks have the oddity than their longest unbeaten streak in regulation is the same length at home and on the road. But to say that the teams setting the records were different would be an understatement.

The 1970–71 Blackhawks set a franchise record that still stands by getting at least one point in each of their first 18 home games. The streak began when the Hawks pummeled the California Golden Seals 5–1 in their home opener on October 11, 1970. Chicago went 16–0–2 (ties with the St. Louis Blues and Minnesota North Stars were the only games in which the Hawks went home without two points) until losing 4–2 to the Los Angeles Kings on January 6, 1971.

The franchise record for the longest unbeaten streak in regulation on the road is also 18 games, though it was spread across two seasons and involved two shootout victories and four shootout losses. It began on March 16, 2012, when the Blackhawks defeated the Dallas Stars at American Airlines Center and didn't end until March 8, 2013, when the Hawks lost 6–2 to the Colorado Avalanche in Denver.

21. d. A total of 44 goaltenders have had shutouts for the Hawks; 11 of them have had exactly one.

The most notable was Hasek, who earned his first NHL shutout by blanking the Toronto Maple Leafs 2–0 on January 9, 1992. Hasek finished with 21 saves. Mike Hudson and Jeremy Roenick scored for Chicago, which had a 44–21 advantage in shots on goal.

It was Hasek's lone shutout before being traded to the Buffalo Sabres that summer.

Emile Francis began his Hall of Fame career as a goalie with the Hawks.

The other Hall of Famer to have exactly one shutout for the Hawks did it more than four decades earlier.

Emile Francis was a star goaltender in juniors in Saskatchewan who came to the Hawks during their down phase. He joined them as a twenty-year-old in 1946–47 and went 6–12–1, then handled the starter's role for most of the 1947–48 season, going 18–31–5 with a 3.39 goals-against average and one shutout, a 3–0 victory against the Bruins at Boston Garden on February 11, 1948.

Like Hasek, Francis was traded before the following season after his shutout. In Francis's case, he was sent to the New York Rangers in a deal that brought goaltender Jim Henry to Chicago. Francis played just 22 games for the Rangers during parts of the next four seasons, going 7–9–5 with a 3.19 GAA—but no more shutouts.

Unlike Hasek, Francis earned induction to the Hockey Hall of Fame for what he did after his playing career. "The Cat" built the New York Rangers into one of the NHL's elite teams in the late 1960s and early 1970s; he also spent time running the St. Louis Blues and Hartford Whalers.

22. a. Whether it was Antti Niemi or Corey Crawford, Chicago's goaltenders finished what they started during the 2010 and 2013 championship runs.

Niemi started all 22 games during the 2010 playoffs and played all but 20 minutes. He finished 16–6 with a 2.63 goals-against average, a save percentage of .910, and two shutouts. Cristobal Huet played one period in a mop-up role.

By the time the 2013 playoffs rolled around, coach Joel Quenneville had decided to roll with Crawford—even though backup Ray Emery had been almost as good during the regular season. Each had a 1.94 goals-against average and three shut-outs; Emery had a 17–1–0 record and a .922 save percentage, and Crawford was 19–5–5 with a .926 save percentage).

Crawford did Niemi one better—not only did he start every game during Chicago's run to the Cup, he played every minute during the playoffs, going 16–7 with a 1.84 GAA and a .932 save percentage.

Crawford got the start on opening night of the 2015 play-offs against the Nashville Predators, but he was pulled after allowing three goals on 12 shots in the first period. Backup Scott Darling started the second period and stopped all 42 shots he faced before Duncan Keith's goal at 7:49 of the second overtime gave the Hawks a 4–3 win.

Quenneville came back with Crawford in Game 2, but the Predators scored six times on 35 shots in a series-tying 6–2 victory.

With the series heading back to the United Center, Quenneville decided that Darling would give the Hawks the best chance to win. He was right: Darling made 35 saves in a 4–2 victory in Game 3, then stopped 50 shots in a 3–2 triple-overtime win that gave the Hawks a 3–1 series lead.

Quenneville called on Darling again in Game 5 at Bridge-stone Arena in Nashville, but the Predators won 5–2 to stay alive.

Darling started again in Game 6 but got the hook 11:16 into the first period after the Predators had taken a 3–1 lead. Crawford made the most of his second chance by stopping all 13 shots he faced and giving the Hawks the chance to rally for a 4–3 victory that closed out the Predators.

It also ended Darling's participation in the playoffs—
Crawford started all 17 games through the next three rounds
and backstopped the Hawks to their third Cup in six seasons.
Darling didn't play again.

23. Minnesota native Mike Karakas, like the rest of the 1937–
38 Hawks, didn't have a very good regular season. However,
Chicago qualified for the Stanley Cup Playoffs despite finishing 14–25–9. Oddsmakers listed them as 100–1 or longer to
win the Cup.

To no one's surprise, the Montreal Canadiens won the
opener of their best-of-three series 6–4. But the Hawks
regrouped, won the second game 4–0, and stunned the Canadiens 3–2 in overtime in the deciding game when Paul Thompson scored at 11:49 of overtime.

Chicago followed a similar script in the Semfinals against
the New York Americans—they lost the first game, then won
the second in overtime. This time Cully Dahlstrom scored at
13:01 of the second overtime for a 1–0 win that evened the
series. Three nights later, Chicago earned a 3–2 victory that
put the Hawks into the Stanley Cup Final against the powerful
Toronto Maple Leafs.

Chicago had finished the regular season with 20 fewer
points than Toronto. But the goaltending of Karakas figured to
give them a chance.

However, Karakas was complaining about a foot injury,
and when doctors checked him out, they found he had a broken big toe.

For Game 1, the Hawks tried to get permission to use
Rangers goaltender Dave Kerr, who was in attendance at Maple
Leaf Gardens. When that was denied, they found minor league

goalie Alfie Moore (legend has it he was located at a local pub a few hours before the game), signed him, and played him in Game 1. After allowing an early goal, Moore was perfect the rest of the way in a 3–1 win.

Maple Leafs boss Conn Smythe was furious, and he successfully lobbied NHL president Frank Calder to prevent the Hawks from using Moore, contending that the signing had been illegal. Calder ruled Moore out of the series, though the Game 1 victory stood. With Paul Goodman in goal for Game 2, the Hawks lost 5–1.

Happily for the Hawks and their fans, Karakas was able to be fitted with a steel-toed skate and took the ice for Game 3. He excelled in a 2–1 win in Game 3 and a series-winning 4–1 victory in Game 4.

However, the Cup was nowhere to be found. Edward Burns of the Chicago Tribune reported that the NHL hadn't even brought the Cup to Chicago because there was so little faith they could win it. "[President Frank] Calder had earlier caused the trophy to be shipped to Toronto," Burns wrote. "It was reportedly on the assurance that a hockey team that harbored eight American-born hockey players as did the Hawks couldn't possibly win the Stanley Cup."

24. d. The Toronto Maple Leafs spoiled the going-away party at Chicago Stadium—twice.

The Maple Leafs were the visiting team on April 14, 1994, when the Blackhawks played their final regular-season game at the Stadium. Each team was already assured of making the Stanley Cup Playoffs, but unlike many end-of-season games, this one was played with a lot of mutual dislike.

There were two fights, 20 minor penalties, 14 power plays, and six goals scored with the extra man. The Hawks led 2–1 in the first period, trailed 4–2 in the second and got even at 4–4 but lost 6–4 when John Cullen scored late in the second period and midway through the third.

The Hawks and Leafs found themselves paired in the opening round of the playoffs, with each team winning its first two home games. But little could Chicago fans have known that Jeremy Roenick's overtime goal that won Game 4 would be their last of the series and the last their team would ever score at the Stadium.

Game 5 was a goaltending duel between Chicago's Ed Belfour and Toronto's Felix Potvin. Mike Eastwood's goal midway through the third period gave Toronto a 1–0 win and a 3–2 lead in the series.

Potvin made sure that Game 6, played on April 28, 1994, would be the last one at the original "Madhouse on Madison." Mike Gartner scored a power-play goal midway through the first period and Potvin made it stand up for his third 1–0 victory of the series, eliminating the Hawks and ending their time at the Stadium.

25. The Hawks were distinct underdogs entering the 1961 Semifinals against the Montreal Canadiens. And why not: The Canadiens had won the Stanley Cup in each of the previous five seasons, made the Final 10 years in a row, and despite the retirement of Maurice Richard had finished first in the regular season, 17 points ahead of the third-place Hawks.

Though Richard had retired, the Canadiens were still loaded with talent. Jean Beliveau was one of the best centers in the league, and Bernie "Boom Boom" Geoffrion became the second player in NHL history to score 50 goals in a season. Defenseman Doug Harvey quarterbacked a power play that had forced the NHL to change the rule that mandated a penalized player serve the full two minutes of his penalty. In goal, Jacques Plante was looking for his seventh Stanley Cup and was 40–11 in the playoffs during the past five seasons.

Montreal had limited Bobby Hull to two goals during the 1960–61 regular season, though the teams split their 14 games, finishing 5–5–4. And though Glenn Hall entered the 1961 playoffs with exactly zero career postseason shutouts, he had led the NHL during the regular season with six.

The Canadiens stretched their playoff winning streak to 11 games with a 6–2 victory in Game 1 at the Forum. But the Hawks evened the series two nights later by rallying for a 4–3 victory.

That set up a Game 3 for the ages at Chicago Stadium.

It was a night for both goaltenders to shine. Murray Balfour put the Hawks ahead with a power-play goal late in the second period. Hall was less than a minute away from his first playoff shutout, but Bill Hay took a penalty with 1:20 remaining and Henri Richard tied the game 1–1 by scoring a power-play goal with 36 seconds remaining in regulation.

The teams battled through one scoreless overtime, and then a second. They were halfway through a third extra period when Montreal forward Dickie Moore was sent to the penalty box—the 26th penalty called by referee Dalton McArthur and the fifth power play awarded after the first overtime.

The game finally ended at 12:12 of the third extra period when Balfour, a former Canadien, took a pass from Stan Mikita and beat Plante for a 2–1 win, setting off an eruption at the Stadium.

There was one more eruption that night: Montreal coach Toe Blake, already upset about what he felt was roughhouse tactics used by the Hawks, especially forward Reggie Fleming, was so livid that he went onto the ice and took a swing at McArthur, registering a glancing blow. Blake was fined $2,000, a significant sum in those days, by NHL President Clarence Campbell.

26. On a team with superstars like Bobby Hull and Stan Mikita and excellent support players such as Ken Wharram, Ron Murphy, Murray Balfour, and Eric Nesterensko, the leading scorer in the playoffs on the Hawks' 1961 Stanley Cup championship team was a defenseman.

But then, Pierre Pilote wasn't just any defenseman.

Pilote was an offensive defenseman before Bobby Orr redefined the term. His offensive style on the blue line was due to the fact that he'd been a center for most of his early years before switching to defense as a teenager. He also didn't play much organized hockey when he was young, but was skilled enough to make the St. Catharines Teepees junior team after switching to defense.

After spending nearly four full seasons with Buffalo of the American Hockey League, Pilote arrived in the NHL late in the 1955–56 season. By 1956–57, he was a regular on the blue line, and two years after that he was a Second-Team All-Star.

Pilote scored six goals, finished with 35 points in 70 games in 1960–61, and also led the NHL with 165 penalty minutes.

But in the playoffs, Pilote led all players with 15 points (three goals, 12 assists) in 12 games. He scored once and had six assists in Chicago's six-game victory against the Montreal Canadiens in the Semifinals, then scored twice and set up six more goals in the Final against the Detroit Red Wings, another six-game victory. Pilote assisted on six of the Hawks' eight game-winning goals in their run to the Cup.

Had the Conn Smythe Trophy existed in 1961, Pilote likely would have won it.

Beginning in 1962–63, Pilote won the Norris Trophy as the NHL's top defenseman for three consecutive seasons and was a First-Team All-Star for five seasons in a row. He retired after the 1968–69 season having played 890 regular-season games in which he scored 80 goals and had 418 assists for 498 points. He was elected to the Hockey Hall of Fame in 1975, and his No. 3 hangs in the rafters at the United Center.

27. All first-place finishes in Hawks history have come since 1966–67, when they finished atop the standings in the final season of the Original Six era. Though Chicago won the Stanley Cup in 1934, 1938, and 1961, the Hawks took home championships despite finishing second (1934) and third (1938 and 1961) during the regular season.

But once the Hawks figured out how to finish first, they got pretty good at it.

Chicago finished on top of the East Division in 1969–70 and had the best record in NHL; the Hawks would have won the Presidents' Trophy had it been awarded back then. In 1970–71, the league moved the Hawks to the West Division with the six teams from the 1967 expansion, and not surprisingly, Chicago came in first in each of the next three seasons, advancing to the Stanley Cup Final in 1971 and 1973.

The Hawks finished second in the West (behind the Philadelphia Flyers) in 1973–74, after which the ever-growing NHL (now up to 18 teams) subdivided further into two conferences and four divisions. Chicago wound up in the Smythe Division, arguably the weakest of the four, and though they came in first in 1975–76 and then from 1977–79, none of those teams finished with more than 87 points in an 80-game season.

The NHL had grown to 21 teams by the time of the next realignment. Beginning in 1981–82, the Hawks, Detroit Red Wings, Toronto Maple Leafs, Minnesota North Stars, and St. Louis Blues were put into the Norris Division. Chicago finished first in 1982–83, 1985–86, 1989–90, 1990–91, and 1992–93; however, their only trip to the Stanley Cup Final while in the Norris Division came in 1991–92, after a second-place finish.

The NHL realigned again in 1993–94, with the Hawks ending up in the Central Division, where life wasn't as easy. They didn't finish first again until 2009–10, when a 52–22–8 record was good for a division title and started the journey that ended with the franchise's first Stanley Cup in 49 years.

Chicago ran away from the pack in the lockout-shortened 2012–13 season, starting 21–0–3 and finishing with a 36–7–5 record that earned the Hawks the Central Division and Western Conference titles as well as the Presidents' Trophy for the best overall record. They went on to win the Stanley Cup again.

28. d. Not surprisingly, numbers below 30 have been the most-used in franchise history. Until the late 1960s, even goalies were almost never given numbers above 30, and it wasn't until the 1980s that skaters were commonly given higher numbers.

But of all the numbers worn by the hundreds of players who've played for the Hawks, the busiest of them all has been No. 6. From the inception of the franchise in 1926 through

2016–17, a total of 57 players have worn No. 6 for at least one game.

No. 6 has a number of attributes when it comes to frequent usage.

First, it's been in almost constant use since the Hawks were born in 1926 and perhaps most important—it's never been retired. Several numbers that would figure to get a lot of traffic (1, 3, and 9, for example) have been retired after being worn for a long time by a single player.

No. 6, on the other hand, seems to be one of those numbers whose wearer often gets traded—and is then issued to his replacement.

The total might be even larger were it not for two players who spent all of their time with the Hawks wearing No. 6.

Forward Paul Thompson came to the Hawks from the New York Rangers in a trade in 1931 and spent the rest of his NHL career with Chicago. He was issued No. 6 when he arrived and wore it for eight seasons, winning championships with the Hawks in 1934 and 1938.

Defenseman Bob Murray, a third-round pick (No. 52) by the Hawks in the 1974 NHL Draft, was issued No. 6 when he made the team a year later. He didn't take it off until he retired after the 1989–90 season, wearing it for 1,008 regular-season games and 112 more in the Stanley Cup Playoffs.

Since Murray gave up No. 6, it's been worn by 21 players, including defenseman Michal Kempny in 2016–17.

In contrast, while there are several (mostly high) numbers that have been worn by just one player through the 2016–17 season, there's only one single-user number guaranteed to stay that way.

Tony Esposito became the first NHL goaltender to be issued No. 35 when he arrived in Chicago after being claimed from the Montreal Canadiens in the 1969 intraleague draft. He was also the first Hawk to wear No. 35 (Nos. 1 and 30, the traditional goalie numbers, had already been issued), and the last. Esposito wore No. 35 until he retired after playing 18 games in the 1983–84 season, and the Blackhawks retired it on November 20, 1988.

29. The Hawks were one of the NHL's best offensive teams for much of the 1960s, but it took until 1968–69 for them to set the franchise record of seven players with 20 or more goals.

Bobby Hull led the way with 58, his highest one-season total in the NHL. Four other players—Stan Mikita, Ken Wharram, Jim Pappin, and Dennis Hull—each scored exactly 30 goals; center Pit Martin scored 23 and forward Doug Mohns had 22.

The Hawks as a team finished second in the NHL with 280 goals scored; however, they also surrendered 246, the most of any team in the East Division, and wound up last despite finishing above .500 with a 34–33–9 record (Chicago would have been second in the West Division, and indeed was transferred to the West in 1970).

The 1981–82 season was an offensive bonanza, the only post-World War II season in which teams combined to score more than eight goals per game. The Blackhawks did their share of scoring, finishing with 332 goals, seventh in the NHL. Al Secord led the Hawks with 44, and Doug Wilson set a team record for defensemen by scoring 39 goals. Denis Savard and Tom Lysiak, the Hawks' top two centers, each scored 32 goals, Grant Mulvey scored 30, Darryl Sutter had 23, and Tim Higgins scored 20. Despite all that offense, the Hawks finished fourth in the Norris Division with a 30–38–12 record, largely because they surrendered 363 goals, the third-highest total in the NHL.

Chicago did tighten up in the playoffs, winning two rounds before falling to the Vancouver Canucks in the Campbell Conference Final.

Some of that cast was still with the Hawks when they had seven 20-goal scorers in 1984–85. Steve Larmer led the Hawks with 46, followed by Savard with 38. No. 2 center Troy Murray scored 26 goals, Curt Fraser had 25, and Wilson scored 22. Rookie and Chicago native Ed Olczyk score 20 goals, as did Sutter.

The Hawks were in the middle of the pack with 309 goals scored, but reduced their goals-against to 299 and finished second in the Norris Division with a 38–35–7 record. As was the case three years earlier, they won their first two rounds in the playoffs before losing the Campbell Conference Final—this time to the Edmonton Oilers in a wild series that saw 69 goals scored in six games.

30. a. The NHL was an eight-team league in 1938, with the Hawks, Boston Bruins, Detroit Red Wings, and New York Rangers in the American Division.

The division was top-heavy: Boston finished first with a record of 30–11–7, and the Rangers were next at 27–15–6. Three of the four teams in the Canadian Division also were over .500. The Hawks grabbed the last playoff berth in their division despite finishing 11 games under .500 at 14–25–9, edging the Red Wings by two points.

No one expected the Hawks to win their best-of-three Quarterfinal series against the Montreal Canadiens, but after losing the opener they won Games 2 and 3. The same thing happened in the Semifinals against the New York Americans— they lost Game 1, then won the next two.

The odd format in use at the time matched the two division winners, the Bruins and Toronto Maple Leafs, in the other Semifinal. Toronto swept the best-of-five series in three games.

At 24–15–9, the Maple Leafs had finished 20 points ahead of the Hawks, but Chicago won the best-of-five Final in four games, becoming the worst regular-season finisher in league history to capture the Cup—a distinction that's still true eight decades later.

31. Chicago goaltenders have faced 91 penalty shots in the regular season since the Hawks entered the NHL in 1926. They've allowed 33 goals (36.3 percent).

Glenn Hall faced 11 in a span of eight seasons, beginning with a save against Larry Leach of the Bruins in a game at Boston Garden on November 8, 1959. He didn't face another one until the 1961–62 season, when he stopped Bruce MacGregor of the Detroit Red Wings on January 31 at Chicago Stadium and J.C. Tremblay at Montreal on February 17. Hall made it 5-for-5 by denying two more shooters in 1962–63—Johnny Bucyk of the Bruins on November 1 at Boston and Murray Oliver of the Bruins at Chicago on January 16.

The first shooter to beat Hall on a penalty shot was Detroit defenseman Doug Barkley, who did it on November 10, 1963. Hall stopped two other penalty shots during the 1963–64 season, denying Forbes Kennedy of the Bruins in Boston on December 22 and Bobby Rousseau of the Canadiens on January 12 at Chicago Stadium.

The final three penalty shots Hall faced all came during the 1966–67 season, his last one with the Hawks. Frank Mahovlich of the Maple Leafs scored at Maple Leaf Gardens on November 22, and Norm Ullman of the Red Wings beat Hall at the Olympia on January 5. Hall stopped the last penalty shot he faced, denying Boston's Bob Dillabough on February 25 at Chicago.

Corey Crawford was in his first full NHL season when he had to face future Hall of Famer Teemu Selanne of the Anaheim Ducks on January 2, 2011, at Honda Center. Selanne finished his NHL career with 684 goals, but didn't score against Crawford that day.

Crawford also stopped the next eight penalty shots he faced during the next couple of seasons, including four in a span of five weeks early in the 2013–14 season. He denied Jonathan Huberdeau at Florida on October 22, TJ Galiardi of Calgary on November 3, Sam Gagner of Edmonton on November 10, and Alex Chiasson at Dallas on November 29.

But four days later, Stars forward Antoine Roussel became the first (and so far only) player to beat Crawford when he scored at the United Center on December 3.

Since then, Crawford has stopped the only penalty shot he's faced—by Jason Zucker of the Minnesota Wild at the United Center on January 11, 2015.

32. d. Fifteen Hawks have combined to score the 16 penalty-shot goals in franchise history. They've come in 71 attempts, meaning that shooters have converted on just 22.5 percent of their opportunities.

Perhaps surprisingly, none of those players is named Stan Mikita or Bobby Hull. Mikita took three penalty shots during

No one in franchise history has taken more penalty shots than Patrick Sharp.

his time with the Hawks and didn't score. Perhaps more amazingly, Hull never attempted a penalty shot during his time with Chicago.

Seven of those attempts were taken by one player. Patrick Sharp seemed to have a knack for drawing penalty shots—he had seven chances in a span of less than six years, from December 22, 2007, to November 17, 2013.

But drawing the penalty shots was one thing; converting them was another. Sharp was stopped on his first six attempts.

He finally succeeded on No. 7, beating San Jose goaltender (and former Chicago teammate) Antti Niemi at the United Center on November 17, 2013.

Jonathan Toews has had just three attempts in his 10 NHL seasons, but he's scored on two of them, making him the only Hawk to convert on more than one penalty shot.

Toews was stopped by Edmonton's Dwayne Roloson at the United Center on March 20, 2009. He scored against Detroit's Jimmy Howard in Chicago on December 30, 2011, and beat Martin Biron of the New York Rangers at Madison Square Garden on February 16, 2012.

Toews and Patrick Kane are the only current Hawks who've taken more than one penalty shot. However, Kane is 0-for-3, failing to score against Marty Turco of the Dallas Stars on January 9, 2008, Miikka Kiprusoff of the Calgary Flames on January 21, 2010, and Al Montoya of the Winnipeg Jets on November 2, 2013.

33. The 1988–89 regular season wasn't one of the Hawks' best. They finished 27–41–12, fourth in the Norris Division, and qualified for the Stanley Cup Playoffs only because the Toronto Maple Leafs managed just 62 points.

One reason for their struggles is that the Hawks had difficulty killing penalties. They allowed an NHL-high 122 power-play goals and finished 19th in the 21-team league on the PK at 74.6 percent.

The one redeeming factor is that the Hawks were the NHL's second-most-dangerous team when it came to scoring shorthanded goals.

Chicago set a franchise record in 1988–89 by scoring 25 goals—two behind the league-leading Edmonton Oilers—while playing a man down.

The shorthanded attack was led by forward Dirk Graham. In his first season as captain, Graham had a career year with 78 points (33 goals, 45 assists) and finished second in the NHL with 10 shorthanded goals (Mario Lemieux of the Pittsburgh Penguins was tops with 13). Graham's 10 shorthanded goals are still a team record.

But he wasn't the only one to put the puck in the net while Chicago was a man down—eight other players had at least one shorthanded goal.

Denis Savard, Graham's predecessor as captain, was second with five shorthanded goals. Wayne Presley was next with three, and Troy Murray scored two.

Five other players—forwards Mike Hudson and Steve Larmer, and defensemen Doug Wilson, Trent Yawney, and Dave Manson—each scored one.

34. The Hawks kept ice crews busy picking up hats during the 1968–69 season, when they established a franchise record with eight hat tricks. Five of the eight came at Chicago Stadium.

Not surprisingly, considering that he scored a franchise-record 58 goals, Bobby Hull led the way with three hat tricks. Two of them came in less than a month, on November 14 at Pittsburgh and December 8 against Boston at Chicago Stadium. The third came at Los Angeles on February 20.

Hull wasn't the only one with multiple hat tricks. Ken Wharram and Jim Pappin each had two. The last one of the season was the best: Center Pit Martin delighted the full house at Chicago Stadium when he scored four goals against the Detroit Red Wings on March 30.

The 1985–86 Hawks matched that achievement, though the hat tricks were a little more spread out. Center Troy Murray had three in less than two months—against Pittsburgh on New Year's Day, against the Minnesota North Stars on February 19, and at Los Angeles eight days later. Five other players—Steve Larmer, Denis Savard, Al Secord, Steve Ludzik, and Curt Fraser—each had one. Secord also had his against Pittsburgh on January 1.

Seven players combined for eight hat tricks in 1989–90. Steve Thomas was the only player with two; Savard, Murray, Secord, Jeremy Roenick, Dirk Graham, and Jocelyn Lemieux each had one. The second one by Thomas, against the New Jersey Devils at the Stadium on March 22, was a four-goal game.

35. b. Charlie Gardiner was the first Hawks goaltender to win the Stanley Cup. Corey Crawford was the most recent. But they have more than that in common.

Gardiner has one attribute that's exclusively his own: He's the only goaltender in NHL history to captain a Stanley Cup championship team. That came in 1934, when the Hawks defeated the Detroit Red Wings 3–1 to win the best-of-five final. Not only was Gardiner the team captain, but he allowed just two goals in the three wins—finishing off the series with a 1–0 shutout in which he was perfect for 90:05 until Mush March scored the Cup-winning goal.

It was one of Gardiner's two shutouts during the 1934 playoffs. He died on June 13, 1934, from a brain hemorrhage brought on by infected tonsils.

Crawford was born on December 31, 1984, exactly 80 years after Gardiner. Like Gardiner, he's a two-time winner of the award given to the goaltenders on the team that allowed the fewest goals in a season (Gardiner won the Vezina Trophy in 1932 and 1934; Crawford won the Jennings Trophy in 2012–13 and 2014–15). Also, each has five playoff shutouts, though no more than two in any one year.

Crawford can't be a captain, and Gardiner never played a Game 7. But the one big thing they have in common is winning the Stanley Cup with a shutout. Eighty-one years after Gardiner blanked Detroit to bring the Hawks their first Cup, Crawford was perfect in a 2–0 victory against the Tampa Bay Lightning in Game 6 of the 2015 Final to give the Blackhawks their third championship since 2010.

36. c. Thanks to their dominance during the 1960s, the Hawks have a winning record against the New York Rangers, one of the three teams that entered the NHL at the start of the 1926–27 season.

Through 2016–17, the Blackhawks were 248–238–98 with three overtime losses against the Rangers, including a 1–0 defeat at the United Center on December 9. Win No. 248 came four days later, when the Hawks outlasted the Rangers 2–1 at Madison Square Garden.

The Blackhawks began their longest unbeaten streak against the Rangers with a 5–3 win at Chicago Stadium on November 18, 1959. The Hawks went 11–0–2 before losing 2–0 at Madison Square Garden on October 19, 1960. They won nine in a row from October 17, 1962, through January 20, 1963, and they had two ties and another win for a 10–0–2 streak before losing 6–1 at the Stadium on February 28, 1963.

One other oddity: Through 2016–17, the teams had never played a shootout.

The next-closest team is the Toronto Maple Leafs; the Hawks are 265–286–96–0 against the Leafs. Chicago won five in a row and 13 of 15 against Toronto from the beginning of 2004 through the 2016–17 season to narrow the margin.

The Hawks' worst record against any of the Original Six is easily their 157–299–103–4 mark against the Montreal Canadiens. However, the Blackhawks have won their past seven games against Montreal and are 9–0–2 since the start of the 2009–10 season. It's their longest active winning and point streak against any member of the Original Six.

37. The tie has gone the way of the wood stick; neither of them can be found in the NHL these days. The Hawks played 814 ties from the time they entered the league in 1926 through the end of the 2003–04 season. The cancellation of the 2004–05 season because of the lockout and the adoption of the shootout when play resumed in 2005–06 have rendered the tie obsolete.

The last tie in franchise history was 2–2 against the Colorado Avalanche in Denver on March 23, 2004. That came two days after the last tie game to be played in Chicago—2–2 against the Phoenix Coyotes.

The arrival of the shootout means the franchise record of 23 ties in a 78-game schedule in 1973–74 should be safe for the ages. The Hawks also set a team record that season by playing 13 ties at home (in 39 games). The road record for ties is 12, set in 1967–68 (the first season after the NHL added six teams in the first expansion) and matched in 1979–80 (another expansion season; the NHL had added four teams from the World Hockey Association in the summer of 1979).

Tony Esposito won 30 or more games eight times with the Hawks.

38. The 22 seasons in which a Chicago goaltender has won 30 or more games have been split among just five players.

On top of the heap is Hall of Famer Tony Esposito, who had 30 or more wins eight times in his 15 seasons with the Hawks. He set a franchise record as a rookie in 1969–70 by going 38–17–8; he was actually the first goaltender in franchise history to win as many as 35 games.

Esposito had seven more 30-win seasons; the last one came when he went 31–22–16 in 1979–80. The most impressive might have been 1971–72, when he went 31–10–6 while playing just 48 games—the fewest by any Chicago goaltender who won 30+ games.

Esposito played in the era when any game that was tied after 60 minutes ended as a tie. Corey Crawford's six seasons have all been played in the overtime/shootout era, giving his win totals a boost. Crawford has won at least 30 games in each of the six full seasons he's played (he was 19–5–0 in the 2012–13 season, which was shortened to 48 games by a lockout). He's done it despite never playing more than 59 games in a season (in 2013–14).

Glenn Hall's victory numbers were held down by the abundance of ties played during his time in Chicago. But he did reach the 30-win mark four times, including three in a row from 1961–62 through 1963–64. The other season was 1965–66, when he matched his career high in wins by going 34–21–7.

Three of the four biggest win totals in franchise history belong to Ed Belfour, the lone 40-win goaltender in Hawks history. He had 43 wins in 1990–91, 41 in 1992–93, and 37 in 1993–94. Ironically, he failed to reach 30 wins in 1991–92, when he helped the Hawks reach the Stanley Cup Final for the first time since 1973.

The only one-time 30-game winner in Blackhawks history was Jocelyn Thibault, who went 33–23–9 in 2001–02. Though Thibault won 238 games in the NHL, this was his only 30-win season and his only winning season with Chicago.

39. Through the 2016–17 season, the Blackhawks' 126 shootouts are tied for sixth among the NHL's 30 teams since the tiebreaker was adopted for the 2005–06 season. They've been among the more successful teams, winning 65 and losing 61; the 65 wins are tied for seventh.

Chicago has scored on 153 of 444 attempts (34.4 percent, ranked tied for eighth). Hawks goaltenders have allowed 146 goals on 443 attempted (67.0 percent save percentage, ranked tied for 20th).

The most successful shooters among the Hawks have been Jonathan Toews and Patrick Kane. Toews leads Chicago with 42 shootout goals, and his 48.3 shooting percentage (42-for-87) is by far the best of any Blackhawks shooter who's taken more than 10 attempts.

No Chicago player has taken more shootout attempts than Kane's 95. He's scored on 40.0 percent (38-for-95), and his 17 game-deciding goals are a franchise record (Toews has 15).

Patrick Sharp is third in attempts (61) and goals (17), though he scored on just 27.9 percent of his attempts.

40. No Chicago forward has had more than five assists during a regular-season game. The Hawks' single-game record is held by defenseman Pat Stapleton, who assisted on six goals in a season-ending 9–5 win against the Detroit Red Wings on March 30, 1969. The six assists also tied the NHL single-game record at the time.

The six-assist night gave Stapleton 50 for the season, setting an NHL record for defensemen (one that wouldn't last long thanks to Bobby Orr, who broke it in 1969–70).

Stapleton wasn't Orr (no one was), but he was one of the best puck-movers of his era, a consistent point producer who teamed with Bill White to form one of the NHL's best defensive pairings. From 1968–69 through 1972–73, he put up 221 points (30 goals, 191 assists) and was plus-150. He was a three-time Second-Team All-Star and helped the Hawks to the Stanley Cup Final in 1971 and 1973.

OVERTIME

It's crunch time! Let's see what you've got left for OT.

1. The Blackhawks thought they had made a huge move in the summer of 1976 when they signed Bobby Orr, who had revolutionized the role of defensemen and led the Boston Bruins to the Stanley Cup in 1970 and 1972. How many games did he play for Chicago? *Answer on page 193.*

2. What surname is the most common on the Blackhawks' all-time player register? *Answer on page 194.*

3. Who led the Blackhawks in scoring in 1960–61, when they won the Stanley Cup for the first time since 1938? *Answer on page 196.*
    a) Bobby Hull
    b) Stan Mikita
    c) Ed Litzenberger
    d) Bill Hay

4. On January 5, 1957, the Blackhawks were part of the first network telecast of an NHL game by a major US television network. Who was their opponent, what was the result, and which network showed the game? *Answer on page 197.*

5. Six Sutter brothers have played in the NHL. How many played for the Blackhawks (and which ones were they)? *Answer on page 198.*

6. Who was the first Blackhawk to have his number retired? *Answer on page 200.*

7. The Blackhawks completed a "worst to first" run by finishing on top of the Eastern Division in 1969–70 by defeating the same team in a home-and-home series on the final weekend of the regular season, costing their opponent a trip to the Stanley Cup Playoffs. Which team did the Blackhawks beat in those two games, and what made the second game especially memorable? *Answer on page 202.*

8. Which of these NHL firsts did not involve the Blackhawks? *Answer on page 204.*
   a) First team to take a chartered flight to a road game
   b) Played in the first afternoon game in league history
   c) First team to take more than 80 shots on goal in a game
   d) First team to pull the goaltender for an extra skater late in the third period

9. Only one person affiliated with the Hawks has won the Stanley Cup and appeared in baseball's World Series (he actually took part in five of them). Who was he? *Answer on page 205.*

10. Which two Hall of Fame goaltenders had their numbers retired by the Blackhawks on the same night? *Answer on page 206.*
   a) Glenn Hall and Ed Belfour
   b) Glenn Hall and Tony Esposito
   c) Tony Esposito and Ed Belfour
   d) Ed Belfour and Charlie Gardiner

You're almost there. But it's time to be at your best. The shootout is coming.

OVERTIME—ANSWERS

1. When Bobby Orr led the NHL in scoring during the 1974–75 season with 135 points (46 goals, 89 assists), he was twenty-seven and on the surface appeared to have many more productive seasons ahead of him.

But Orr had always had trouble with his knees, and a knee injury sustained in training camp limited him to 10 games and 18 points for the Boston Bruins during the 1975–76 season, after which he became a free agent.

Bad knees or not, the Bruins wanted to keep Orr, and he wanted to stay with them. Boston's original offer reportedly was $4 million for 10 years ($400,000 a season sounds ludicrous now, but at the time it was astronomical). The knee problems persuaded the Bruins to revise their offer, cutting down on the money but adding an 18.5 percent ownership stake in the team.

Sounds like a great offer, doesn't it? Orr might well have agreed, but his agent, Alan Eagleson, had other ideas.

Eagleson and Hawks owner William Wirtz were tight, and Wirtz wanted Orr, figuring that adding the best defenseman in NHL history to a team that included stars like Stan Mikita and Tony Esposito would give him the best team in the NHL.

Orr wound up signing a reported five-year, $3 million contract with the Black Hawks on June 24, 1976. He contended later that Eagleson had withheld information from him. Orr, who for years had put all of his financial interests in Eagleson's hands, said he was unaware he could have had an ownership stake in the Bruins had he re-signed with Boston.

He looked like his old self three months later, earning MVP honors while leading Team Canada to victory in the first Canada Cup tournament, a best-on-best event. It was especially sweet for Orr because he'd been unable to play in the Summit Series against the Soviet Union four years earlier.

But 12 games into the regular season, Orr had to have a specialist flush bone particles out of the knee. He returned to the ice in January 1977, but was able to play just eight more games before concluding that he could not continue. He finished with 23 points in the 20 games in which he did play.

Instead of flying around Chicago Stadium, Orr had knee surgery that kept him out for the rest of the 1976–77 season and all of the 1977–78 season. He was able to start the 1978–79 season, but managed to play all of six games before informing the Black Hawks that he couldn't play any more. On Nov. 8, 1978, after scoring six goals and finishing with 27 points in 26 games with Chicago, Orr called it a career at the age of thirty. The Hockey Hall of Fame waived its usual three-year waiting period and inducted Orr on September 12, 1979.

2. The Blackhawks have had seven players named Brown and seven named Smith, but the winner for the most-used name in franchise history is Wilson. Eight players with that name have seen action for the Hawks.

The best of the eight was defenseman Doug Wilson, who played 938 games with Chicago, scoring 225 goals and finishing with 779 points. Wilson won the Norris Trophy as the NHL's best defenseman in 1981–82, when he scored 39 goals and finished with 85 points. Wilson was a First-Team All-Star in 1981–82, a Second-Team All-Star in 1984–85 and 1989–90, and represented Chicago in six NHL All-Star Games as well as Rendez-Vous 87, a series between All-Star teams from the NHL and the Soviet Union. Doug Wilson is tops among all defensemen in franchise history in goals and points.

No other Wilson comes close to Doug's success or longevity as a member of the Blackhawks. No. 2 in games played and points was another defenseman, Behn Wilson, who scored 39 goals and had 144 points in 262 games with Chicago, which acquired him from the Philadelphia Flyers on June 8, 1983. He hit double figures in goals in each of his first three seasons with Chicago, including a 13-goal, 50-point performance in 1985–86. But he had to sit out all of the following season because of back problems. He put up six goals and 29 points in 1987–88, but never played again after that, as the back problems forced him to retire a few months before he turned thirty.

Johnny Wilson was a forward who came to the Blackhawks in an eight-player trade with the Detroit Red Wings on May 27, 1955, not long after becoming a four-time Stanley Cup champion. Wilson scored a career-high 24 goals in 1955–56 and had career-bests of 30 assists and 48 points with Chicago the following season. But he wound up being sent back to Detroit on July 23, 1957, in a trade that brought goaltender Glenn Hall to Chicago.

Johnny Wilson's younger brother, Larry Wilson, also started with the Red Wings and came to the Black Hawks in a trade on August 12, 1953. After playing 21 games during three seasons while trying to break into a loaded lineup in Detroit, Larry Wilson had a career year in 1953–54 with nine goals and 42 points in 66 games. He dropped to 12 goals and 23 points in 1954–55, then played just two games in 1955–56 before being sent to Buffalo of the American Hockey League. He was ultimately sold to Buffalo on August 12, 1957, and played with the Bisons though 1967–68, then spent two more seasons with Dayton of the International Hockey League before finally retiring a few months before his 40th birthday.

The first Wilson to wear a Black Hawk uniform was Cully, a right wing who had not played in the NHL since 1922–23 when he came to Chicago for the 1926–27 season. At age thirty-four, Cully Wilson had eight goals and 12 points in 39 games for the Hawks. It was his last season in the NHL, although he spent another five seasons in the minors before hanging up his skates.

The other three Wilsons spent only a short time with the Blackhawks. Rik Wilson, a defenseman who was a first-round draft pick by the St. Louis Blues in 1980, played the last 14 games of his NHL career with Chicago in 1987–88, scoring four goals and finishing with nine points. He bounced around between Europe and the minor leagues until the early 1990s.

Roger Wilson played seven games for the Blackhawks in 1974–75, finishing with two assists. Robert Wilson played one game in 1953–54.

3. d. His name has been forgotten by all but the most fervent Hawks fans (like you, since you're reading this book), but the leading point producer on that 1960–61 championship team was neither Bobby Hull nor Stan Mikita. Nor was it captain Eddie Litzenberger.

No, the man at the top of the scoring list for those Black Hawks was a second-year center named Bill "Red" Hay, who had won the Calder Trophy as the NHL's top rookie in

1959–60 and led Chicago in 1960–61 with 59 points (11 goals, 48 assists).

Hay found himself on the "Million Dollar Line" between Bobby Hull and Murray Balfour. There are worse ways to make a living (though Hay is quick to note that the sobriquet of "Million Dollar Line" had nothing to do with how much the three linemates were making).

"I said to Bobby, 'You've been trying to go through everybody on the team, end to end, and it's not doing you any good,'" Hay said in a 2015 interview. "'It's simple; Murray will battle in the corners, I'll get the puck and fool around with it, I'll get it to you in front of the net, and you shoot it in. That's all we have to do.' It worked good."

Hay spent most of his time in Chicago with Hull on his left until deciding to leave the NHL and join the family oil business. He came back for a while in 1965–66, but left the NHL for good when he was put into the Expansion Draft in 1967. The St. Louis Blues took Hay and offered him more money that he'd ever made in Chicago, but he hung up his skates at age thirty-one.

Hay was as good in the oil business as he'd been on the ice. He also stayed involved in hockey, helping to bring the Atlanta Flames to Calgary and later becoming president and part-owner of the Calgary Flames. He later went on to spend 33 years in various roles with the Hockey Hall of Fame, which inducted him as a builder in 2015.

4. The Blackhawks and New York Rangers took to the ice at Madison Square Garden on January 5, 1957, with something new in the arena: network television cameras. Though "Hockey Night in Canada" was already a fixture north of the border, network television in the United States had never been interested in showing the NHL to its audience.

However, CBS was on hand at the Garden that day, with Bud Palmer handling the play-by-play chores and Fred Cusick providing analysis and doing interviews.

The Rangers won that game 4–1. Glen Skov's goal early in the third period was the only one of Chicago's 32 shots to beat Gump Worsley. Andy Bathgate scored the game's first goal and assisted on two others for the Rangers against Al Rollins.

It was the first of a 10-game package to be shown on CBS that season. The Hawks played three more times, all at Chicago Stadium. They lost 3–2 to the Detroit Red Wings on January 19, defeated the Boston Bruins 6–5 on February 16, and edged the Red Wings 4–3 on February 23.

The four US-based teams reportedly received $100,000 from CBS for the TV rights; however, the players got nothing. CBS continued to televise a package of afternoon games for the next three seasons

According to *Sports Illustrated*, the NHL dropped CBS after the 1959–60 season because the owners didn't want the new Players' Association to gain a financial cut of the TV deal.

5. It's hard to conceive that six brothers could all make the NHL (and play in the league at the same time). But so it was with the six Sutter brothers from Viking, Alberta. All six had solid NHL careers, and at one time or another, four of the six wore red, black, and white.

The first one to join the Hawks was Darryl, the only one they actually selected in the NHL Draft. Though he expected to be taken in the second or third round, Darryl lasted until the Hawks took him in the 11th round (No. 179) in 1978.

Sutter was so displeased with being selected that low in the draft that he opted to spend a season playing in Japan. After returning, he scored 35 goals and was named the American Hockey League rookie of the year in 1979–80, earning a call-up from the Hawks. He scored twice in eight NHL games and never looked back.

Darryl made the Hawks in 1980–81 and stunned everyone by scoring 40 goals as a rookie, finishing fourth in balloting for the Calder Trophy as the NHL's top rookie. He never approached that total again but had at least 20 goals in each of the next four seasons despite playing through a spate of injuries.

In 1984–85, he scored 12 goals in 15 playoff games, breaking a team record held by Bobby Hull. But continuing knee problems forced him to retire after the 1986–87 season at age twenty-nine. He finished his NHL career with 161 goals and 279 points in 406 games, all with the Blackhawks.

But the Hawks weren't without a Sutter when they reconvened for the 1987–88 season. Duane Sutter, the third brother and also a forward, came to Chicago after eight seasons with the New York Islanders; he was a role player on the Isles' four Stanley Cup-winning teams from 1980–83. Duane had the feistiness typical of the Sutters, but he didn't have the offensive skills that Darryl did. Duane had scored 13–20 goals in each of his previous six seasons with the Islanders, but he had a total of 18 goals and 50 points in 184 games during three seasons with the Blackhawks, though he did help them advance to the Campbell Conference Final in 1989 and 1990.

Duane also had a career-high of 214 penalty minutes in 1988–89 and 156 in 72 games in 1989–90, his final NHL season.

Brent Sutter joined Duane with the Islanders in 1981–82 and played on three of their four championship teams. He was named New York's captain in 1987, when Denis Potvin relinquished the "C." Brent scored at least 21 goals (and as many as 42) during 10 full seasons with the Islanders before being acquired by the Blackhawks early in the 1991–92 season. He helped the Blackhawks advance to the Stanley Cup Final in 1992 and remained with them though the 1997–98 season as a checking center who could contribute offensively, finishing his time in Chicago with 76 goals and 219 points in 417 games.

In 1993–94 and the early part of 1994–95, the Blackhawks had two Sutters. Rich Sutter, chosen by the Pittsburgh Penguins with the 10th selection in the 1982 NHL Draft (six picks behind twin brother Ron), was acquired by the Blackhawks in the 1992 intraleague waiver draft. He put up 12 goals and 26 points for Chicago in 1993–94 and extended his streak of 100-PIM seasons to nine with 108. But after Rich went without a point in 15 games during the lockout-shortened 1994–95 season, the Blackhawks traded him to the Tampa Bay Lightning.

6. Of all the great players who've worn Blackhawks' colors, none has worn them longer (and few, if any, better) than Stan Mikita. The Hockey Hall of Famer spent all 22 of his NHL seasons with Chicago (1958–80), setting numerous franchise records.

Mikita is the franchise leader in games played (1,394), assists (926), and points (1,467), and he's second to longtime teammate Bobby Hull in goals (541). He was also among the first players in the NHL to wear a helmet.

That's why, prior to a game against the Washington Capitals on October 19, 1980, Mikita became the first player in franchise history to have his number retired. A banner with his No. 21 and the years "1959–80" was raised to the rafters behind the west goal at Chicago Stadium in honor of Mikita, whose entire professional career was played with the Blackhawks. He never spent a day in the minor leagues.

Joining Mikita for the on-ice ceremony was his wife, Jill, as well as their four children, Meg, Scott, Jane, and Christopher. Also on hand for the celebration was Joe Mikita, Stan's uncle, who adopted the 8-year-old and brought him from Czechoslovakia to St. Catharines, Ontario.

The packed house at the Stadium gave Mikita a two-minute standing ovation, then roared again when he donned his No. 21 for one last time.

Mikita thanked his former coaches, Rudy Pilous and Billy Reay, as well as longtime general manager Tommy Ivan. Though he saluted all of the teammates he played with during his time in Chicago, he noted that "I really only had five linemates —Kenny Wharram, Ab McDonald, and Doug Mohns from the days of the Scooter Line, and I'm also proud to say

No one wore a Hawks uniform longer than Stan Mikita.

I played with a couple of plowhorses—Cliff Koroll and John Marks."

But perhaps the biggest thank-you was saved for Uncle Joe, who "gave me the greatest commodity in life. He took me out of a Communist country and gave me something I think we're all striving for: He gave me my freedom. I'd like to pay tribute to the greatest guy I know: my pop."

7. Despite the fact that Bobby Hull set an NHL record in 1968–69 by scoring 58 goals and finished second in the scoring race with 107 points, 10 more than teammate Stan Mikita, the Black Hawks came in last in the East Division with a 34–33–9 record and 77 points (to be fair, they'd have finished second in the West). The biggest problem was defense. The Hawks were second in the NHL in scoring with 280 goals, but were by far the worst defensive team in the East. Chicago allowed 246 goals, 25 more than the next-worst team in the conference.

But the arrival of rookie goaltender Tony Esposito for the 1969–70 season changed all that. Though the Black Hawks dropped from 280 goals to 250, Chicago cut its goals against from 246 to 170—basically one goal per game.

Chicago and the Boston Bruins entered the final weekend of the regular season all even with 95 points in the battle for first place in the East. All six teams in the East finished with home-and-home series; the Blackhawks had arguably the toughest assignment—back-to-back games against the Montreal Canadiens, beginning with a Saturday night game at the Forum. Not only were the Canadiens the two-time defending Cup champions, they needed the points to stay ahead of the New York Rangers in the battle for the final playoff berth.

With Esposito playing against his former team, the Hawks rolled to a 4–1 victory at the Forum to stay even with the Bruins, who defeated the Maple Leafs 4–2 in Toronto. The Canadiens got a break when the Detroit Red Wings defeated the Rangers 6–2 at the Olympia, assuring themselves of third place.

The Rangers and Red Wings played Sunday afternoon in a nationally televised game at Madison Square Garden; not only did New York need to win, it needed at least five goals to have a chance to catch Montreal—at the time, goals for was the second tiebreaker, and the Canadiens had a five-goal lead on New York.

With the Red Wings having nothing to play for, the Rangers came out flying, grabbing a 9–3 lead. Coach Emile Francis even lifted goaltender Ed Giacomin late in the third period and replaced him with an extra attacker in an effort to generate more goals.

New York's 9–5 win meant that the Canadiens and Black Hawks each had something to play for in their season finale. Yvan Cournoyer put Montreal ahead with a power-play goal midway through the first period, but goals by Jim Pappin and Pit Martin gave the Hawks a 2–1 lead after one period. Bobby Hull made it 3–1 early in the second, but Montreal's Jean Beliveau scored two minutes after Hull to cut the margin to 3–2.

Martin scored twice in the third period to complete his hat trick and give Chicago a 5–2 lead. With a victory no longer a realistic possibility, Montreal coach Toe Blake followed the example set by Francis earlier in the day and pulled his goaltender for an extra attacker. Instead, the Hawks hit the empty net five times, with each goal triggering another roar of approval. Eric Nesterenko, Cliff Koroll, Dennis Hull, Bobby

Hull, and Gerry Pinder each scored into the vacated net, and the five empty-net goals turned the game into a 10–2 blowout that completed Chicago's worst-to-first season and kept the Canadiens out of the playoffs.

8. c. The Hawks were the first team to take a chartered airplane flight to a road game; they did it March 18, 1940, when they flew to Toronto for their first-round playoff series against the Maple Leafs.

Chicago played the first afternoon game in NHL history on March 19, 1933. The Detroit Red Wings came to Chicago Stadium and defeated the Hawks 4–3.

The Hawks were the first team to pull the goaltender in favor of a sixth attacker on March 16, 1941, when coach Paul Thompson lifted rookie goaltender Sam LoPresti (it didn't help; Toronto won 3–0).

The Black Hawks were involved in the game that saw a team set the NHL record for shots on goal in a game, but they were the party of the second part. On March 4, 1941, LoPresti took the ice for the Black Hawks against the Bruins at Boston Garden and faced a barrage like no NHL goaltender has seen before or since.

LoPresti made 27 saves in the first period, 31 in the second, and 22 more in the third. Boston goaltender Frank Brimsek (who, ironically, came from the same hometown as LoPresti—Eveleth, Minnesota) made 18 saves on 20 shots.

It wasn't until late in the game that Boston's Eddie Wiseman knocked a rebound past LoPresti to give the Bruins a 3–2 win.

The 83 shots faced and 80 saves are still NHL single-game records more than 75 years later.

LoPresti played 1½ seasons with the Hawks, finishing with a 30–38–6 record and a 3.13 goals-against average. He joined the US Navy after the 1941–42 season and did not return to the NHL after World War II; in fact, he nearly didn't return at all after the merchant ship he was aboard was torpedoed off the coast of Africa.

Sam's son, Pete LoPresti, was also an NHL goaltender, appearing in 175 games (43–102–20) with the Minnesota North Stars and Edmonton Oilers.

9. To say that Bill Stewart was versatile would be an understatement.

Stewart wanted to be a pitcher and signed with the Chicago White Sox, but an offseason injury helped to keep him out of the major leagues. He became a minor-league manager, and later an umpire, working his way up to the National League in 1933.

He remained with the NL through the 1954 season, capping his career by working in his fifth World Series. He also umpired four All-Star Games.

But Hawks fans remember him for a different reason.

During baseball offseasons, the Massachusetts native had coached high school and college hockey teams. In 1928, he became the NHL's first US-born referee. He remained in that job through 1941, with the exception of the 1937–38 and 1938–39 seasons.

Major Frederic McLaughlin, the Hawks' owner, hired Stewart as his coach for the 1937–38 season. It didn't look like a great move when the Hawks went 14–25–9 in the regular season. But that was still good enough to make the Stanley Cup Playoffs, and in perhaps the most unlikely run to a championship in NHL history, Chicago defeated the Montreal Canadiens, New York Americans, and Toronto Maple Leafs for the second Cup in franchise history.

Alas for Stewart, the Hawks couldn't build on their championship. They were 8–10–3 with the season nearing the midway point and had won just three of their previous 17 games when McLaughlin fired him.

"I don't think I had it coming," Stewart said after being canned. "I thought when this team won four straight at the start of the season that it was playing over its head. I still think so. The Hawks are not that good. Since then, injuries and bad breaks have cost us games."

By the following autumn, Stewart had returned to his role as an NHL referee when he wasn't umpiring National League games.

Stewart's connection to the NHL was reinforced when his grandson, Paul Stewart, went from a role player to a longtime referee.

10. b. Four generations of Chicago goaltenders have found their way into the Hockey Hall of Fame (maybe someday Corey Crawford will make it five), but only two of them have had their numbers retired by the Hawks—and those retirements happened on the same night.

Glenn Hall, aka "Mr. Goalie," and Tony Esposito had their numbers raised to the rafters of Chicago Stadium on November 20, 1988.

Hall spent a decade with the Hawks, backstopping them to the Stanley Cup in 1961 and finishing with a record of 275–229–106, including 51 shutouts. He started every game during the run to the Cup in '61.

Hall, one of the pioneers of the "butterfly" style of goal-tending that's common today, had perhaps the strangest ritual in NHL history. Because of nerves, Hall usually became physically ill either before or during the game. Often, he'd quietly throw up before the game and/or during intermission. "I always felt I played better if I was physically sick before the game. If I wasn't sick, I felt I hadn't done everything I could to try to win," Hall once said.

No one could accuse Hall of faking illness or injury. He showed up for work every night—literally. Hall played in 502 consecutive regular-season games; that's one record no one is ever likely to break. More amazing: He did it without wearing a mask.

The Hawks let Hall go to the St. Louis Blues in the 1967 Expansion Draft, and it took a couple of years for their next franchise goaltender to arrive.

But unlike Hall, who had established himself with the Detroit Red Wings before being traded to Chicago, the Black Hawks got Esposito for free—well, he did cost them the waiver fee of $25,000 teams paid for taking a player in the intraleague draft, but that turned out to be some of the best money the Black Hawks ever spent.

Esposito came over from the Montreal Canadiens, where he had played 13 games in 1968–69, and was an instant star, finishing with a 38–17–8 record and 2.17 goals-against average. He won the Calder Trophy and the Vezina Trophy as a rookie, when he helped the Blackhawks finish first in the East Division after coming in last a year earlier.

Like Hall before him, Esposito was one of the rare practitioners of the butterfly—they were oddities in an era when the stand-up goaltender was the role. Detractors kept saying that opposing shooters were sure to fill the net because he dropped to the ice so much.

But "Tony O" kept putting up wins and shutouts for 15 seasons in Chicago, earning 418 of his 423 career victories with Chicago, as well as 74 of his 76 NHL shutouts. The Hawks never failed to make the Stanley Cup Playoffs during Esposito's time in Chicago, and he led them to the Final in 1971 and 1973, though the Canadiens spoiled the party each time.

SHOOTOUT

You've battled your way to the end without flinching. You've probably learned a few things about your favorite team that you might not have known.

Now it's time for the most challenging questions. Let's get to the shootout!

1. The Blackhawks' litany of great goaltenders is a lengthy one. But only one netminder in franchise history has played in more than one game without giving up a goal. Who is this masked man? *Answer on page 211.*

2. The Blackhawks' appearance in the 2017 Stanley Cup Playoffs marked the 62nd time in their 90 NHL seasons that the franchise has qualified for the postseason. They've played 22 of the other 29 NHL teams at least once during that time. They've failed to win a series from four of those 22 teams, but against which one have they failed to win so much as a single game? *Answer on page 212.*

3. It's not unusual to have players who are teammates in junior hockey wind up as teammates in the NHL. But the Black Hawks of the early 1970s had a rarity for that era—they had two players who had played for the same US college hockey team (at a time when few players with NHL aspirations took the college route) and joined the Hawks together. Who were these two Hawks, and where did they go to school? *Answer on page 213.*

4. Every franchise has some "one-hit wonders"—players whose NHL career consists of a single game—and the Blackhawks are no different. During the 1991–92 season, the Blackhawks gave a one-off appearance to a longtime minor-league goaltender. Who was he, why did he get the chance, and how did he fare in his one NHL game? *Answer on page 215.*

5. Only one person has played for three Chicago pro teams—the Blackhawks, Bulls, and White Sox. Who is this unique performer? *Answer on page 217.*

That's it. The final question. Time to tally up the numbers and get the final score.

SHOOTOUT—ANSWERS

1. A total of 80 players have played goal for the Blackhawks, and 68 have seen action in more than one game. But the only one of those 68 who didn't allow a goal was Chris Clifford, who played in two games for Chicago four seasons apart.

Clifford was chosen by Chicago in the sixth round (No. 111) of the 1984 NHL Draft despite going 16–28–0 with a 4.89 goals-against average in his first season with Kingston of the Ontario Hockey League.

He was in his second season with Kingston when he was summoned by the Black Hawks and got into a game against the Buffalo Sabres on March 8, 1985. The Sabres had torched Murray Bannerman for seven goals in two periods at Memorial Auditorium, and Clifford, at age eighteen, went out for the third period and stopped all eight shots he faced in what ended as a 7–2 victory for the Sabres.

Clifford went back and finished the 1984–85 season with Kingston, then played two more seasons in the OHL. His most notable accomplishment was scoring a goal during a game on January 7, 1987.

He turned pro after the 1986–87 season and joined the Saginaw Hawks of the International Hockey League, where he went 9–7–2 with a 4.19 GAA in 22 games. Clifford got a second brief trip to the NHL with the Blackhawks midway through the 1988–89 season and got into a game at Buffalo on January 12, 1989. He did not see a shot or allow a goal in a 4:10 stint.

When the Blackhawks didn't re-sign him that summer, Clifford joined the Pittsburgh Penguins as a free agent. But he never saw any action with the Penguins, instead splitting his time between the International Hockey League and the ECHL before retiring after the 1993–94 season.

Clifford's final line in the NHL reads: 2 games played, 24 minutes, eight shots, eight saves, and a GAA of 0.00. Perhaps ironically, he never had a GAA better than 3.87 in any of the three minor leagues in which he played.

Three other goaltenders, Tom Cook, Christian Soucy, and Moe Roberts, each played a small portion of one game with the Blackhawks and did not allow a goal.

2. The Black Hawks had the misfortune to run into the New York Islanders twice in a three-season span during the late 1970s, when the Isles were building a team that went on to win four consecutive Stanley Cups from 1980–83.

The Hawks were swept by New York in their best-of-three Preliminary Round series in 1977. They didn't get any help from the fact that the two games were played at Nassau Coliseum; Chicago Stadium, which normally would have been the site of Game 2, was hosting a Led Zeppelin concert. The Black Hawks wore their home uniforms and got the last line change that goes along with playing in their own building. But the game was played on Long Island and the Islanders, who had won the opener 5–2, played as the visiting team in their own building and defeated Chicago 2–1 despite a 33-save performance by Tony Esposito.

Two years later, the Black Hawks ran into the Islanders in the 1979 Quarterfinals after New York had dethroned the Montreal Canadiens as regular-season champions. The Hawks got to play some home playoff games against the Islanders this time, but the result was no better than it had been in 1977. After 5–2 and 1–0 losses on Long Island, the Black Hawks lost 4–0 and 3–1 at Chicago Stadium. Islanders star Mike Bossy personally outscored the Blackhawks 5–3 in the series.

Chicago has also gone 0–1 in playoff series against the Phoenix (now Arizona) Coyotes and 0–2 against the Buffalo Sabres and Colorado Avalanche. But they managed to win at least one game against each of those three teams.

3. US college hockey in the late 1960s and early 1970s wasn't the pathway to the National Hockey League that it's become decades later. But for Cliff Koroll and Keith Magnuson, the road to the NHL went straight through the University of Denver.

Koroll and Magnuson had been friends since their days in youth hockey. Each had dreams of playing in the NHL, but they eschewed the more conventional route of junior hockey and played for Denver, winning an NCAA championship in their senior year.

The duo cracked the lineup in Chicago during the 1969–70 season. Magnuson quickly became a fan favorite because of his willingness to fight anyone. He was a rugged defensive defenseman who finished his NHL career with 14 goals, 125 assists, and 1,442 penalty minutes in 589 NHL games.

Koroll, a reliable two-way forward, had more goals in his rookie season (18) than Magnuson scored in his entire NHL career. After an early-season hat trick, Koroll found a home as the right wing on Stan Mikita's line; he replaced Kenny Wharram, who had been forced to retire because of a heart condition.

Keith Magnuson helped the Hawks get to the Stanley Cup Final in 1971 and 1973.

Mikita and Koroll became roommates as well as linemates, with Koroll doing a lot of the dirty work in the corners and becoming one of the best two-way forwards in hockey. He was a five-time 20-goal scorer for the Hawks and had a career-best 33 goals in 1972–73, helping Chicago advance to the Stanley Cup Final for the second time in three seasons.

Just as they came into the NHL together, Magnuson and Koroll left it together. They hung up their skates in 1980 (as did Mikita). But their time together was not over. Magnuson was named coach shortly after his retirement and brought in Koroll as one of his assistants. Koroll outlasted Magnuson, who was let go in 1982, and remained with the Hawks as an assistant for seven years.

Koroll also worked for a time in the front office before going on to a successful business career. But much of his time was spent helping grow one of Magnuson's pet projects, the Chicago Blackhawks Alumni Association, especially after Magnuson's death in an auto accident in 2003.

"His death was the worst thing to happen—not just to me, but everybody who knew this wonderful, funny, unselfish man, husband, and parent," said Koroll, who delivered the eulogy at his best friend's funeral. "Not an hour goes by that I don't think of him."

4. One of the surprise stars of the 1992 Winter Olympics in Albertville, France, was an unknown minor-league goaltender named Ray LeBlanc. The twenty-seven-year-old from Fitchburg, Massachusetts, stood on his head and got the United States into the medal round, something that hadn't happened since the "Miracle on Ice" team won it all at Lake Placid in 1980. In the pre-NHL years, the US Olympic Team was still a hodgepodge of lower-level pros and amateurs.

With LeBlanc in goal, the United States was the only team to emerge from the preliminary round without a loss. The Americans' dreams of a gold medal ended with a semifinal loss to the Unified Team (made up of players from the former Soviet Union) and they wound up fourth after a 6–1 loss to Czechoslovakia in the bronze medal game.

Still, the chance to play for his country at the Olympics was a career boost for LeBlanc, who had spent most of the previous decades in such hockey hot spots as New Haven, Flint, Saginaw, Fort Wayne, and Indianapolis. Though the Blackhawks signed him as a free agent in 1989, it looked like the only way LeBlanc would get into a Hawks game was with a ticket.

But the combination of a superb Olympic showing and Chicago's need to make a goalie available in the upcoming expansion draft (Tampa Bay and Ottawa began play in the Fall of 1992) combined to provide LeBlanc with his 60 minutes of fame. With the lowly San Jose Sharks, then in their second NHL season, coming to Chicago Stadium on March 10, 1992, LeBlanc got the call.

Wearing No. 50, LeBlanc took the ice and acquitted himself quite well. He got plenty of offensive support, with five players each scoring a goal, and earned a 5–1 victory by making 21 saves, allowing only a third-period goal to Mike Sullivan (the same Mike Sullivan who later coached the Pittsburgh Penguins to the Stanley Cup in 2016 and 2017).

It was a taste of the big time for a player who'd spent more than a decade riding the buses in the minor leagues. But that's all it was—a taste. While the chance to start an NHL game was certainly a reward, it was also a way for the Blackhawks to prevent the loss of Ed Belfour or Dominik Hasek in the expansion draft that summer.

LeBlanc soon found himself back with Indianapolis of the International Hockey League. Ironically, he did make his way back to Chicago—but with the Chicago Wolves of the IHL, not the Blackhawks. He spent four seasons with the Wolves, then played for Flint of the United Hockey League and

Jacksonville of the ECHL before hanging up his pads following the 1999–2000 season, having played more than 36,000 minutes of professional hockey, just 60 of them in the NHL.

"Sure there was discouragement, but I look back on my career and I'm blessed," he told *Sports Illustrated* in 2012. "Through hockey, there was always a roof over my head and food on the table. It doesn't matter if it was one game or a thousand games in the NHL. I got to do something that I dreamed about when I was a kid."

5. Well, we didn't say the person in question was actually a player—only that this person played for those three Chicago teams.

That's exactly what organist Nancy Faust did.

Though Faust is best known as the longtime organist for the Chicago White Sox, for whom she played from 1970 through 2010, Faust also provided the musical soundtrack for the NBA's Chicago Bulls from 1975–84, and for the Blackhawks from 1984–89, meaning that she got to play Chicago Stadium's famed 3,663-pipe Barton pipe organ for Hawks fans.

After 1989, she confined her skills to the White Sox, making the move with the team from Comiskey Park to what's now known as Guaranteed Rate Field in 1991.

Though Faust didn't get to play for a Stanley Cup winner, she did get to celebrate a World Series championship with the White Sox in 2005 before retiring five years later.

PHOTO CREDITS

First period

1. **Stan Mikita**
   Francesca from Chicago
   License: CC BY-SA 2.0, https://creativecommons.org
     /licenses/by-sa/2.0/legalcode
   Source: https://commons.wikimedia.org/wiki/File:Stan
     Mikita.jpg

2. **Marian Hossa**
   Photo by Lisa Gansky.
   License: CC BY-SA 2.0 https://creativecommons
     .org/licenses/by-sa/2.0/legalcode
   Source: https://commons.wikimedia.org/wiki/
     File:Marian_Hossa_-_Chicago_Blackhawks.jpg

3. **Dave Bolland**
   Photo by Anna Enriquez.
   License: CC BY 2.0 https://creativecommons.org
     /licenses/by/2.0/legalcode
   Source: https://commons.wikimedia.org/wiki/File:Dave
     Bolland(5442431814).jpg

4. **Michael Frolik**
   Photo by Anna Enriquez.
   License: CC BY 2.0, https://creativecommons.org
     /licenses/by/2.0/legalcode

Source: https://commons.wikimedia.org/wiki/File:
   Michael Frolik (5442403102).jpg

5. Andrew Ladd
Photo by Matt Boulton.
License: CC BY-SA 2.0, https://creativecommons.org
   /licenses/by-sa/2.0/legalcode
Source: https://commons.wikimedia.org/wiki/File:
   Andrew Ladd.jpg

Second period

1. Billy Reay
Chicago Black Hawks / National Hockey League - ebay.com

2. Jonathan Toews
Photo by Anna Enriquez.
License: CC BY 2.0; https://creativecommons.org/licenses
   /by/2.0/legalcode
Source: https://commons.wikimedia.org/wiki/File:
   Jonathan Toews (5441828977).jpg

3. Coach Joel Quenneville
https://www.flickr.com/photos/swimfinfan
License: https://creativecommons.org/licenses/by-sa/2.0
   /legalcode
Source: https://commons.wikimedia.org/wiki/File:Coachq
   -cup-2015.jpg

4. Corey Crawford
Photo by Anna Enriquez.
License: CC BY 2.0, https://creativecommons.org/licenses
   /by/2.0/legalcode

Source: https://commons.wikimedia.org/wiki
/File:Corey Crawford (5442402202) (cropped1).jpg

5. Patrick Kane
Photo by Lisa Gansky.
License: CC BY-SA 2.0, https://creativecommons.org
/licenses/by-sa/2.0/legalcode
Source: https://commons.wikimedia.org/wiki/File:
Patrick Kane - Chicago Blackhawks.jpg

Third period

1. Bobby Hull
Courtesy of Dave Stubbs

2. Niklas Hjalmarsson
Photo by Lisa Gansky.
License: CC BY SA 2.0; https://creativecommons.org
/licenses/by-sa/2.0/legalcode
Source: https://commons.wikimedia.org/wiki/File:
Niklas_Hjalmarsson_-_Chicago_Blackhawks.jpg

3. Emile Francis
Source: http://news.google.com/newspapers?id=-NFTA
AAAIBAJ&sjid=uzgNAAAAIBAJ&pg=5528,30014
75&dq=emile+francis&hl=en

4. Patrick Sharp
Photo by Anna Enriquez.
License: CC by 2.0, https://commons.wikimedia
.org/w/index.php?curid=54010031
Source: https://commons.wikimedia.org/wiki/File:
Patrick_Sharp_(5441821669).jpg

5. Tony Esposito
By Chicago Blackhawks / NHL

Overtime

1. Stan Mikita
Courtesy of Dave Stubbs

Shootout

1. Keith Magnuson
Chicago Black Hawks - ebayfrontback, Public Domain
Source: http://www.ebay.com/itm/1973-Keith-Magnuson
-Chicago-Blackhawks-8-x-10-B-W-Original-Photo
-/360875033507?pt=Vintage_Sports_Memorabilia
&hash=item5405d403a3